Secret Weapon

Secret Weapon: High-value Target Teams as an Organizational Innovation

By Christopher J. Lamb and Evan Munsing

Institute for National Strategic Studies
Strategic Perspectives, No. 4

Series Editor: Phillip C. Saunders

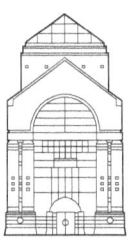

National Defense University Press
Washington, D.C.
March 2011

First printing, March 2011

For current publications of the Institute for National Strategic Studies, please go to the National Defense University Web site at: www.ndu.edu/inss.

Contents

Executive Summary

This study argues that interagency teams were a major catalyst in turning around the Iraq War, and that they will disappear from America's arsenal unless the knowledge base supporting the innovation can be secured. Most explanations credit the dramatic reduction in violence in Iraq between 2007 and 2008 to new U.S. leadership, the surge in U.S. forces, and/or U.S. financial support to Sunni tribal leaders. In contrast, we argue that the United States employed an underappreciated organizational innovation—interagency teams—to put insurgent clandestine organizations on the defensive and give population security measures a chance to take effect.

By the end of 2004, Special Operations Forces (SOF) were using interagency high-value target teams in Iraq that were tactically successful—even awe-inspiring—but they were not making a strategic difference. They would hit a cell and it would reconstitute, and sometimes inadvertent collateral damage would occur that alienated the local population. Meanwhile, Army commanders in Mosul, Tal Afar, and Ramadi demonstrated that the insurgency could be beaten with organizations and tactics capable of conducting classic counterinsurgency warfare. They targeted insurgents and terrorists with sufficient discrimination to put them on the defensive, while population-centric security measures and influence operations pacified the broader population. The SOF and Army commanders used a kind of collaborative warfare that involved three separate innovations, each of which required interagency collaboration and all of which ultimately had to merge into a unified approach.

The first innovation was network-based targeting. This meant charting the clandestine terrorist and insurgent cells and their immediate supporters in order to attack them, but also using all-source intelligence to reveal the local environment, its social networks, and key decisionmakers and their motivations. The second innovation was the fusion of improved all-source intelligence with operational capability. Having intelligence and operations working together in common space on a sustained basis produced persistent surveillance, improved discrimination, and better decisionmaking. The third innovation was the integration of counterterrorist and counterinsurgency efforts and the proliferation of this model. All three innovations—networked-based targeting, fusion of intelligence and operations, and counterterrorist-counterinsurgency integration—required unprecedented collaboration between diverse departments and agencies and between SOF and conventional forces. Together, these innovations set the stage for the dramatic reversal of the security situation in Iraq in 2007.

We explain the performance of the interagency high-value target teams using 10 variables often cited in organizational literature as important determinants of team success. The qualitative assessments offered by personnel with direct experience on the teams unanimously underscore the importance of common purpose, clearly delegated authorities, small size and collocation, and a supportive organizational context. Teams that did not develop a sense of common purpose were not able to override interference from parent organizations. When, initially, interagency teams did not benefit from clearly delegated authorities, their performance suffered. When the teams later were clearly empowered, their performance improved, but the issue of ambiguous authorities was a constant source of tension and a major reason for the fragility of the teams' performance. The ability of the teams to learn also was important. SOF did a better job of assessing the second- and third-order effects of their operations and made a greater strategic contribution after learning the importance of expanding their collaboration to include conventional forces. Finally, because departments and agencies could hamstring team performance by withholding support, cajoling parent organizations for support was a major preoccupation of senior leaders in Iraq.

The U.S. experience with interagency teams justifies several broader observations.

Organization matters. The interagency teams, when working well, took counterterrorism efforts (leadership targeting) to an unprecedented level of efficacy, permitting great pressure to be applied to enemy leadership and clandestine cells. Interagency teaming also was essential to the success of population-centric counterinsurgency efforts pioneered in Mosul and then applied more broadly by General David Petraeus and Ambassador Ryan Crocker. Both the interagency high-value target teams and the interagency approach eventually embraced by conventional forces demonstrate that how the national security system is organized for complex missions matters greatly.

Interagency teams are not well understood or respected. Some SOF leaders and practitioners note the importance of interagency teams, but they are not otherwise extolled in the literature and certainly have not been codified in military doctrine as best practices. Moreover, there previously had been no attempt to understand what performance variables best explain their effectiveness and why they were fragile and subject to periodic downturns in productivity. The varying performance of different teams (and of the same teams at different times) underscores the need to better understand the prerequisites for successful teams so the United States can more consistently exploit their potential.

Greater attention to data collection and a multidisciplinary approach to analysis of interagency teams are needed. Currently, there is little institutional interest in such research or desire to track which personnel have benefited from experience on interagency teams or led them well.

The interagency high-value target teams in Iraq have attracted surprisingly little attention and study—in effect serving as a "secret weapon" in the fight against terrorism. Bob Woodward's

60 Minutes exposé on a new operational capability in Iraq doing so much to turn the war around was widely misinterpreted as referring to a mysterious technology of some sort. Instead, he was referring to the interagency high-value target teams where SOF collaborated with diverse intelligence organizations. When the high-value target teams and integrated conventional force commands collaborated tactically, they produced quick and powerful results. When Petraeus and Crocker used collaborative warfare more broadly in pursuit of a consistent counterinsurgency strategy, the situation in Iraq turned around dramatically. Collaborative organizations are not only powerful but also cost effective. In comparison with new weapons or reconstruction funding, interagency teams cost next to nothing and can be used almost anywhere. However, collaboration is a difficult force to harness and institutionalize. We hope this research contributes to the preservation of collaborative warfare by explaining how the interagency teams actually worked and what it might take to ensure their continued effectiveness.

Introduction

I'd like to think that we're adaptable. But I don't know that we are. And a lot of the things I see . . . have not changed since I came here in 2003. We put a new name on something and called it something else, but it's the same thing. The one revolution I've seen between then and now is the joint interagency task force.
—Senior Department of Defense intelligence official covering Iraq, 2008[1]

In 2007, after most informed commentators had given up hope for any progress, the United States succeeded in turning around the deteriorating situation in Iraq. Civilian deaths dropped 70 percent from the previous year,[2] and violence would decrease another 80 percent the following year.[3] Most explanations for this dramatic reversal focus on several factors: new U.S. leadership with a new strategy emphasizing protection of the Iraqi population; the five-brigade surge in U.S. forces (and arrival of newly trained Iraqi forces); and U.S. financial support to Sunni tribal leaders who swung their militias in support of U.S. forces.[4] A few sources cite another factor, however. They assert that the United States employed a new weapon against the insurgents and terrorists, one so powerful that it awed the President and thrilled hard-bitten intelligence professionals closely monitoring developments in Iraq.[5] Christened *collaborative warfare* by one proponent, the new capability reportedly captured or killed enemies so fast that it put their clandestine organizations on the defensive and gave population security measures a chance to shift public support to government forces.[6]

Unlike the unmanned drones that kill terrorist suspects from afar, the new capability was not a high-profile technological breakthrough, but rather an underappreciated organizational innovation. This study argues that this organizational innovation was a major catalyst in turning around the Iraq War, and that it may disappear from America's arsenal as quickly as it appeared unless the knowledge base supporting the innovation can be secured and institutionalized. We hope to contribute to the preservation of this capability by examining how the new organizations actually worked and what it might take to ensure their continued effectiveness.

Revelations about the work of these new interagency organizations have intermittently appeared in the American press and trade journal articles, but they remain underappreciated and poorly understood. A range of interagency teams and "fusion cells" have been used to fight terrorism. The type that captured press attention and that is examined here is an interagency mechanism developed in the field to identify, track, and defeat terrorists and insurgent networks. These teams combine military and civilian personnel from a variety of government agencies as well as civilian contracting companies. An article in the *Washington Post* describes a seamlessly coordinated effort involving multiple government agencies in which:

> the CIA [Central Intelligence Agency] *provides intelligence analysts and spycraft with sensors and cameras that can track targets, vehicles or equipment for up to 14 hours. FBI* [Federal Bureau of Investigation] *forensic experts dissect data, from cellphone information to the "pocket litter" found on extremists. Treasury officials track funds flowing among extremists and from governments. National Security Agency staffers intercept conversations or computer data, and members of the National Geospatial-Intelligence Agency use high-tech equipment to pinpoint where suspected extremists are using phones or computers.[7]*

Washington Post reporter Bob Woodward asserts that the interagency teams were at least as important as the surge in American troops in decreasing violence in Iraq between 2007 and 2008, and arguably more so.[8] He contends that the use of such interagency teams is comparable, in military terms, to the invention of the tank or the airplane.[9] A few government sources also claim the teams constitute "a revolutionary way of fighting modern day warfare," but otherwise this remarkable capability goes unheralded, submerged among more general and frequent calls for improved civil-military cooperation.[10]

After interviewing conventional and Special Operations officers with service in Afghanistan and Iraq, reviewing unclassified portions of official reports and studies, and analyzing the chronology of key events leading up to and through the improved security situation in Iraq in 2007, we believe the interagency teams used to target enemy clandestine networks were a major, even indispensible, catalyst for success. It is harder to make the case that they constitute a revolutionary capability because their stellar performance was irregular and fragile, subject to periodic breakdown and atrophy. These limitations just make it all the more important to understand the factors that contributed to the success of high-performance interagency teams so they can be made more consistently effective in the future. There is a vast amount of organizational literature on teams,[11] some historical experience with interagency teams in the national security system, and some notable recommendations for their expanded use.[12] Yet there is little current research on interagency teams and to date little effort by the national security system to codify lessons learned from the experience.[13] This unfortunate dearth of interest increases the likelihood that a giant leap forward in America's ability to fight its enemies and protect the homeland will be squandered, much as previous interagency innovations have been lost and never replicated.[14] The lack of attention is also quite surprising given the broad, current consensus that the United States needs to improve interagency collaboration.

Interagency Coordination and Cross-functional Teams

The need to improve collaboration among national security organizations is a common refrain in national security literature and one echoed by senior leaders. The current administration, like the previous two, acknowledges that the "United States must integrate its ability to employ all elements of national power in a cohesive manner" to succeed in the 21st century.[15] Virtually every major national security study over the past decade or so agrees and has identified inadequate interagency cooperation as a glaring systemic deficiency.[16] Yet little progress has been made toward correcting this shortcoming. The attacks on September 11, 2001, spurred some structural and procedural innovations to facilitate interagency collaboration, but as Secretary of Defense Robert Gates recently observed, "Despite improvements in recent years, America's interagency toolkit is a hodgepodge of jerry-rigged arrangements constrained by a dated and complex patchwork of authorities, persistent shortfalls in resources, and unwieldy processes."[17]

The National Security Council would seem the most likely organ to direct and improve national security integration, but it has only the power to advise the President.[18] The President has to forge interagency cooperation by convening coordination committees, designating a particular agency to lead an interagency effort, or utilizing "czars" who rely on prestige and the aura of delegated Presidential authority to accomplish interagency coordination. These approaches regularly fail, and when they succeed it is often because of extraordinary leadership and good fortune—factors to be welcomed but not relied upon. Thus, as one notably successful practitioner of interagency arts recently lamented, there is still "no effective, consistent mechanism that brings a whole interagency team to focus on a particular foreign policy issue."[19] As a result, progress is often personality- and situation-dependent, slow to materialize, and fleeting.

Cross-functional teams are a recommended but seldom tried institutional remedy for improving interagency collaboration.[20] Simply stated, they use team dynamics to combine diverse bodies of relevant functional expertise to solve problems. For decades, businesses and nongovernmental organizations have used cross-functional teams, designed "as an overlay to an existing functional organization."[21] These teams create links among an organization's departments, allowing more flexible decisionmaking at lower levels within the organization and the ability to tackle complex problems that demand the rapid integration of diverse bodies of expertise. For example, a car company might create a new automobile prototype by forming a team consisting of representatives from the design, engineering, manufacturing, marketing, and sales departments.

Currently, committees are the prevalent cross-departmental mechanism employed in the national security system. Committees are distinguished by having little or no authority and few resources. Members of the committee are not accountable for success or failure, and their main goal tends to be simple coordination or information-sharing. Teams, on the other hand, reputedly solve problems faster than committees[22] and have better organizational learning mechanisms,[23] broader external networks that give them access to multiple functional areas and perspectives,[24] increased capability for innovative solutions,[25] and a better division of labor utilizing specialists from diverse backgrounds.

Although infrequently used within the government, teams are not unknown to the national security system. Experiments with teams have produced promising results, but these successes have been neither pursued nor institutionalized.[26] This case study examines whether the experience of interagency high-value target teams substantiates the assertion that the use of teams in the national security system would provide better, more dynamic problem-solving, especially in a complex and rapidly evolving environment. We look at the case of interagency teams pursuing important enemy leaders and examine a set of variables that might explain good team performance. We begin by adopting the variables used by the Project on National Security Reform to explain good team performance:[27] clear mandates, authorities, resources, team composition (size, location, and tenure), and team culture, training, and rewards.[28] To provide context for assessing the value of these variables independently and collectively, we first summarize how the use of interagency teams grew in post-9/11 counterterrorist operations until they reached their apex of effectiveness in Iraq between 2005 and 2007, and we then examine the variables that most affected their performance.

Experimentation with Cross-functional Teams in Afghanistan

U.S. operations in Afghanistan from 2001 to 2003 highlighted both the value of and problems involved in creating effective interagency teams, as well as the key role SOF would play in interagency teams in the war on terror (see figure 1). SOF are arguably more comfortable with interagency cooperation than conventional forces for several reasons, not least of which is that they have a long history of using cross-functional teams. The basic Army Special Forces 12-man "A-team" consists of a leader, a second in command, and two men for each of the five Special Forces functional areas: weapons, engineering, medical,

communications, and operations and intelligence (see figure 2). A-teams and other SOF units fuse intelligence and operations planning, unlike conventional military staff systems where these two functions are kept separate. Because SOF work in dynamic, unpredictable environments, their leaders and planners must be aware of the changing environment "in enough time and detail to employ their forces effectively."[29] This necessitates constant communication

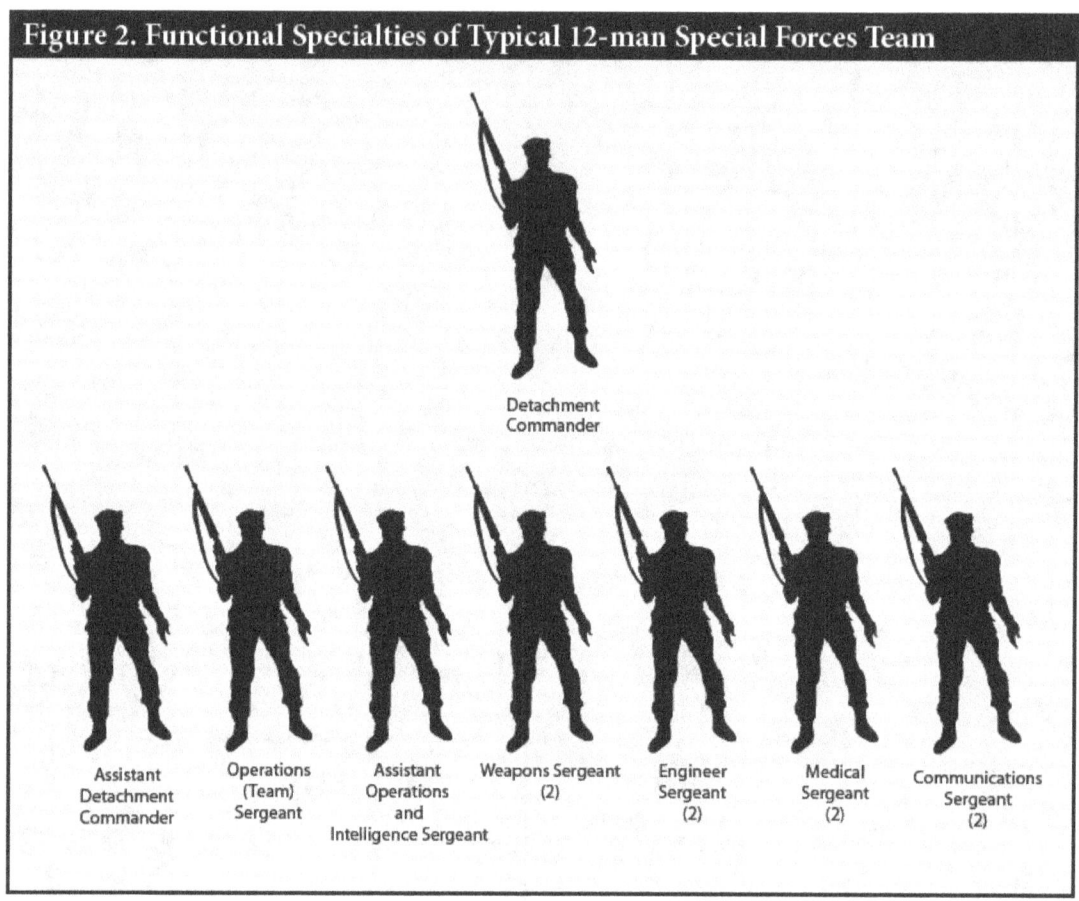

Figure 2. Functional Specialties of Typical 12-man Special Forces Team

Detachment Commander

Assistant Detachment Commander

Operations (Team) Sergeant

Assistant Operations and Intelligence Sergeant

Weapons Sergeant (2)

Engineer Sergeant (2)

Medical Sergeant (2)

Communications Sergeant (2)

between those responsible for collecting intelligence and those planning and deciding on the course of action.

Moreover, SOF have a history of working with interagency partners with different functional specialties. These factors facilitated working relationships among the SOF units that entered Afghanistan after the attacks on September 11 and the Intelligence Community staff officers who preceded them.[30] Army Special Forces that typically work closely with indigenous military forces, U.S. Air Force combat controllers, and other SOF units that specialize in the most difficult direct action missions, along with Intelligence Community personnel, formed tactical ad hoc "pilot teams" on the ground to coordinate their efforts. By combining their individual and organizational expertise, including unique capabilities such as access to the Intelligence Community's satellite network and American airpower, these ad hoc teams were able to engineer the swift victory of the Northern Alliance over the Taliban. They accomplished their mission in a matter of months with fewer than 500 of America's best military and intelligence operators.[31] An officer with experience on these interagency pilot teams explained their agility: "The intent is to tailor the force for the situation, so it's never quite the same, but it's always small, it's always cross-functional, it's always the best of the best working in it."[32]

The use of interagency teams was also seized upon at the operational level by General Tommy Franks, then Commander of U.S. Central Command. Franks requested permission to form an "interagency coordination cell" in October 2001, and by late November Joint Interagency Task Force–Counter Terrorism (JIATF–CT) was operating out of Bagram Air Base under the name of Task Force Bowie. Opening the doors to as many interagency partners as it could recruit, the military was joined by the FBI, CIA, Diplomatic Security Service, Customs Service, National Security Agency (NSA), Defense Intelligence Agency and its Defense Human Intelligence Service, New York's Joint Terrorism Task Force, and the Departments of Justice, Treasury, and State, among others.[33] These personnel formed an analysis team that worked to unravel Taliban and al Qaeda networks. In keeping with the SOF practice of intelligence operations fusion,[34] the interagency analysis team was directly supported by Special Operations Forces.[35] JIATF–CT racked up some notable successes, detaining several senior al Qaeda leaders as well as creating a border security program for Afghanistan based on biometric identification.[36] Other commands were also setting up JIATFs to facilitate their efforts in the war on terror.[37]

As American military and civilian efforts in Afghanistan expanded from 2001 to 2002, so did the use of interagency teams. Troop levels increased more than sevenfold—from 1,300 in November 2001 to 9,700 in December 2002[38]—and commanders wanted to replicate the successful interagency partnerships that had spearheaded the American response. However, since other SOF personnel were in short supply, Army Rangers (the largest Special Operations Command component) were tapped to staff the new interagency cross-functional teams (CFTs). The Rangers were joined on the CFTs by deployed personnel from the FBI, CIA, NSA, U.S. Agency for International Development (USAID), and later the Department of State. Led by Ranger battalion executive officers who had received some prior training in interagency management, the CFTs assumed regional responsibilities for collecting intelligence, targeting enemies, and distributing funds. The teams depended on voluntary participation, and their authorities were limited. They had no explicit mandate to utilize personnel or assets from other departments and agencies that were working in their areas.[39] Even their relationship with other military forces was tenuous. Conventional forces were not yet interested in collaborating with other agencies, and Special Forces preferred autonomy while working with indigenous forces.[40] The CFTs could not direct units inside their area of operations unless those units were formally attached to the team, and even simple deconfliction with the diverse U.S. presence in the area occasionally proved difficult. [41]

Between 2002 and 2003, additional funding from the Joint Special Operations Task Force headquarters and interagency partners allowed CFTs to use some of the intelligence analysts and operators who were coming to Afghanistan in increased numbers to create "all-source fusion cells" to work in conjunction with the CFTs. These fusion cells, described as "CFTs on steroids" but focused on intelligence,[42] expanded the teams' capability to collect, analyze, and disseminate intelligence on enemy networks coming from various agencies and in various forms (such as signals and human intelligence). They began supplying the larger conventional forces that were deploying into Afghanistan with all-source intelligence. Conventional forces were wary of working too closely with SOF (and therefore with the CFTs) and were not culturally inclined toward intelligence-operations fusion. However, they did appreciate and use the fusion cells as all-source intelligence staff support.[43] Thus, the conventional forces maintained the traditional bifurcation of intelligence and operations in the conventional military command and staff structure.

In some cases, the reduction in close collaboration among the disparate players that accompanied the arrival of conventional forces seriously compromised the success of operations. Operation *Anaconda*, the near-disaster that was designed to trap a group of hard-core Taliban and al Qaeda fighters close to the Afghanistan-Pakistan border in March 2002, is a case in point (see figure 3). As one compelling study of that operation concluded, coordination problems began in January 2002 when operations in Afghanistan shifted suddenly from "a geographically dispersed SOF-centric force with decentralized planning to a large, concentrated, conventional ground force with operations requiring detailed functional component planning."[44] The conventional force commander was not well equipped or trained to handle the integration of so many actors and failed to use the full spectrum of interagency intelligence capabilities that were offered, resulting in fratricide, underuse of air assets, and poor tactical intelligence.[45]

By 2003, interagency constructs in Afghanistan had demonstrated that they could make important contributions but also that their value was constrained by several factors. First, SOF practiced intelligence-operations fusion, which could better exploit interagency contributions, but conventional forces did not. They preferred using interagency intelligence fusion cells that did a good job of providing multispectrum intelligence but that were separated from operations. This functional separation created knowledge gaps and delayed operations. Even within the SOF interagency teams, military members would often find themselves at cross-purposes with their teammates from the Intelligence Community. A constant tension existed between the SOF desire to hit targets as soon as possible and the Intelligence Community's predilection to

Figure 3.

U.S. Special Forces help Northern Alliance troops away from CIA-operated Mi-17 Hip helicopter during Operation *Anaconda*

protect sources and collect information for as long as possible.[46] Furthermore, SOF teams that captured or killed high-value targets were weak in exploitation and analysis. They did not have the means or inclination to collect and exploit evidence from the targets and their immediate surroundings that would help reveal the inner workings of the enemy networks. The FBI had provided training to the military in sensitive site exploitation since 2002 and had trained its own agents to work on sensitive sites with the military since 2003, but there were simply not enough agents to go around. High-value target teams that were not lucky enough to have resident FBI agents approached site exploitation in a haphazard way, "tossing evidence collected from several sites into one sack and then dumping it onto the S2's [intelligence officer's] desk and saying 'Here you go.'"[47] An undisciplined approach reduced the value of the intelligence by displacing and contaminating it, and available data often was not applied to the larger task of revealing the terrorist network supporting the target.

Finally, there was a significant difference between the mission focus of the high-value target teams and the rest of the coalition military forces responsible for stability operations. An officer with experience in both types of units remembered that the high-value target teams' focus on taking down terrorist leadership meant that they "broke stuff up and the general purpose forces [conventional forces] had to pick up the pieces."[48] The collateral political and sometimes physical damage complicated counterinsurgency efforts and made conventional force commanders less willing to collaborate with the high-value target teams. The more numerous conventional forces that were in daily contact with the population were a valuable source of intelligence and operational assistance, but the tension between them and SOF impeded overall progress against the terrorists. CFTs were not notably successful in bridging the divide between SOF and conventional forces, but they persisted and in fact would migrate from Afghanistan to Iraq,[49] where they continued to provide all-source intelligence and worked with conventional forces and public affairs to help control negative public reactions to SOF operations against high-value targets. By 2005, however, the CFTs would generally be replaced by intelligence fusion cells.[50]

Thus, by early 2003, the United States had pioneered the use of diverse interagency teams in Afghanistan at the operational and tactical levels but had not yet identified and removed several major impediments to achieving high levels of effectiveness. There were still too many fissures between all the actors required for an integrated effort: between SOF and conventional forces, between SOF and diverse intelligence disciplines, and between conventional forces and the intelligence fusion cells. CFTs were voluntary and irregular organizations, and the general consensus was that their output was useful but inconsistent and did not have a major impact. If there was any inclination to sort through the experience and improve upon it, it was lost in the rush to prepare for a different kind of war in Iraq. But after a lightning-quick victory against Iraqi conventional forces, the war effort bogged down amid insurgent and terrorist attacks in the summer of 2003. In the years ahead, U.S. forces would find a way to employ highly effective interagency teams, but not before enduring much costly trial and error.

Top-down Emphasis on Interagency Teams in Iraq

Experience in the war on terror and in Afghanistan in particular had demonstrated the value of interagency collaboration, but many leaders remained wary of cooperating too closely across departmental lines or uncertain of how best to do so (see table 1). At the national level, there was a robust and successful interagency effort to unravel global terrorist finance systems,[51] a goal pursued by a range of interagency groups before coalescing in 2004–2005 around U.S. Central Command's Threat Finance Exploitation Unit, supported by the U.S. Special Operations Command.[52] These task forces analyzed and dismantled the external networks that fund terrorists by tracking money flows through formal financial systems, hawala, trade-based value transfers, and the physical importation of cash into Iraq from neighboring countries.

Table 1. Interagency Bodies Involved at Strategic, Operational, and Tactical Levels

Strategic Level	Threat Finance Exploitation Unit
	National Security Council staff
	LTG Douglas Lute (War Czar)
Operational Level	Joint Interagency Coordination Group
	Joint Interagency Task Force
	Joint Special Operations Task Force
	Combined Joint Special Operations Task Force
Tactical Level	Pilot Team
	Task Force
	Cross-functional Team
	Fusion Cell
	Intelligence Fusion Cell

Their success required the combined efforts of the intelligence, law enforcement, financial, military, and diplomatic communities within the U.S. Government and the international community.[53]

At the operational level, the variety of interagency task forces pioneered in Afghanistan migrated to Iraq, along with their merits, flaws, and varying degrees of effectiveness (see figure 4). For example, Multinational Force–Iraq JIATF was created shortly after the invasion in 2003. Based at Camp Victory in Baghdad, it was initially tasked with identifying and tracking terrorist funding in Iraq. Its mission was abruptly changed in November 2004 to the identification of former Ba'athists who posed a threat to the occupation, at which point its name changed to JIATF–Former Regime Elements. Although numerous agencies participated (including the FBI, Bureau of Immigration and Customs Enforcement, Defense Human Intelligence Service, and members of foreign intelligence and security services[54]), rapid turnover in leadership, a confused sense of purpose,[55] a lack of authority and resources,[56] and personality conflicts among the team members ruined its effectiveness, and the task force slowly unraveled, underlining the fragility of interagency teams and the care with which team leaders and members must be selected.[57] On the other hand, some interagency teams like JIATF–West, which was tasked with dismantling the networks that allowed foreign fighters to enter Iraq from the Middle East, Asia, and Africa, racked up major successes. JIATF–West worked with other agencies outside Iraq to

Figure 4.

U.S. Army (David Russell)

U.S. Special Forces review map data while conducting operation

staunch the flow of terrorists entering Iraq, or at least to provide actionable intelligence to other interagency teams in the country to eliminate the threat when the terrorists arrived.[58]

At the tactical level, even greater interagency teamwork was evident. The importation of the CFT concept to Iraq, sometimes by the direct migration of teams to Iraq from Afghanistan,[59] and through the leadership of a general officer in the U.S. Special Operations Command whom we will refer to in this research as "General Smith" to meet Pentagon security requirements. Smith had served as chief of staff on a SOF task force with interagency representation in Afghanistan and created such a task force in 2002 to coordinate intelligence, SOF, and other Department of Defense activities in Afghanistan.[60] Smith became the pivotal figure in creating SOF support for interagency performance in Iraq. By late summer and early fall of 2003, he had three SOF headquarters with interagency representatives in Baghdad,[61] and his interagency connections would only grow stronger.

Smith and his task force leaders knew passing intelligence between organizations and between analysts and operators often resulted in delays and "dropped balls" that let the enemy escape. He wanted constant, seamless tracking of clandestine enemies, which was impossible without all-source intelligence working in direct cooperation with his operators. He also knew he could not command such assets and would have to woo them instead. With characteristic SOF determination and an unusual degree of diplomacy, Smith managed to get buy-in from a wide range of department heads. He asked senior officials from other departments and agencies to join his headquarters staff. He attracted support from the Intelligence Community through personal contacts and made a point of demonstrating how much they were valued as members of the team. Eventually, he was able to bring in a senior Intelligence Community official as his deputy for interagency operations, which raised the angst of Pentagon lawyers who worried about violating the statutory basis of the military chain of command.[62] He later obtained an Ambassador from the Department of State, an organization otherwise conspicuously absent at a tactical level.[63] Over time, he expanded the number of interagency staff members working with him and succeeded in bringing on Senior Executive Service–level representatives from many departments, which helped ensure his interagency teams got the level of support they needed. Smith was so successful at getting interagency support that a single task force in Iraq had over 100 embedded interagency members.[64]

By force of personal example, General Smith created an unprecedented sense of interagency unity and ensured the personnel on his teams were given appropriate support from their parent organizations.[65] He made sure everyone from every agency felt that they were part of the team. He was assiduous in recognizing contributions from interagency partners, often calling out individuals by name in meetings and video teleconferences, which could be held as often as four or five times a week.[66] He followed the time-honored practice of praising in public and admonishing in private.[67] Smith also took extraordinary steps to ensure interagency teams worked well in the field. He hand-picked SOF officers at the O–3 and O–4 levels to lead the interagency high-value target teams based on his assessment of their personalities, and if they failed, he brought them back early.[68] He was looking for Soldiers who could lead a diverse group of people over whom they had little direct authority. These Soldiers built interagency teams that created unprecedented levels of collaboration, allowing them to track and destroy al Qaeda's networks in Iraq. Smith delegated authority to these teams but cautioned them that an operation gone wrong would undermine their credibility, which, he often told them, "brings us freedom of action."[69]

By the end of 2004, General Smith and his interagency high-value target teams were the only U.S. forces in Iraq wholly committed to being on the offensive.[70] They were tactically successful—even awe-inspiring—which helped cement interagency support for their activities, but they were not making a strategic difference.[71] They would hit a cell and it would reconstitute, and sometimes there would be inadvertent collateral damage that alienated the local population. The team metrics were all quantitative—number of takedowns—with no qualitative assessment of impact on the terrorists' operations or team counterinsurgency efforts.[72] But this would change thanks to a few local commanders who innovated in the face of pending defeat.

Bottom-up Experimentation with Interagency Teams in Iraq

Task Force Freedom in Mosul

The rapid influx of foreign fighters into Iraq and overall deterioration of security in mid- to late 2004 spurred new organizational innovations in the field—most notably in Mosul, where U.S. forces forged the first interagency team[73] dedicated to counterinsurgency at the tactical level. The 101st Airborne Division had occupied Mosul in 2003,[74] but U.S. forces there were reduced to just a single Stryker brigade in early 2004: Brigadier General Carter Ham's Task Force Olympia. As security in Mosul began to deteriorate, Ham began reaching out to the other government agencies in the area in an effort to increase the effectiveness of his small unit. He hosted regular Friday meetings to engage as many interagency partners as best he could.[75] However, with less than a third of the troops and half of the reconstruction funding of the 101st, and with insufficient intelligence collection and analysis teams, Task Force Olympia was limited in what it could accomplish. Worse, it was repeatedly ordered to conduct operations outside of its area of operations.[76] Security in Mosul continued to deteriorate even as the regional command transferred to Task Force Freedom, based on the 1st Brigade, 25th Infantry Division Stryker Brigade Combat Team (SBCT) led by Colonel Robert Brown, in fall 2004.

Task Force Freedom was nearly as undermanned as Task Force Olympia, and its forces were similarly dissipated. One of the brigade's battalions was dispatched to help with the assault on Fallujah. Ironically, large numbers of insurgents escaping the assault on Fallujah, known as "squirters," moved to Mosul.[77] There, they systematically eliminated the local police force, terrorized the population, and precipitated the Battle of Mosul of November 8–16, 2004, during which they gained control over significant portions of the city.[78] Task Force Freedom was in dire need of more manpower to protect a province of some 7 million people. By the end of 2004, the brigade was carrying out 18 attacks a day on insurgents,[79] but the insurgents were escalating their efforts as well with an average of over 21 attacks per day.[80] In response, Task Force Freedom's staff began to work more closely with other military and interagency partners in the area (see figures 5a and 5b). They reached out to civilian partners, members of the Intelligence Community, Special Forces, and units from General Smith's interagency high-value target teams.

(Smith's SOF units were generally referred to in theater simply as "The Task Force," but to avoid confusion with other task forces and Special Forces, we refer to them in this publication as the "SOF Task Force." We refer to the combined SOF Task Force personnel and interagency personnel as the "interagency high-value target teams.")

Personnel in Task Force Freedom used a number of means to increase collaboration among their partners in Mosul. To begin, they expanded and refined General Ham's Friday roundtable discussions as a forum for sharing information and ideas. The brigade operations officer, who was also a former Special Forces officer, identified this as a basic but fundamental breakthrough in facilitating cooperation. Previously, "everyone had their own lane, their own target deck, but they weren't synchronizing their work." Now, as full partners in the security process, the representatives of the other government departments and agencies were delighted to have the chance to work closely with the military.[81] The collocation of the task force headquarters, the brigade headquarters, and their all-source intelligence fusion cell in the Arrow Head Palace in East Mosul facilitated integration. It also helped that the State Department headquarters for Northern Iraq was in the palace compound, which was itself within a few miles of the Special Forces and Ranger base. Personal friendships between some of the Special Forces, Ranger, and Stryker commanders, harkening back to previous shared military experiences, also improved communication. As the Task Force Freedom staff increased in size, they were able to push out analysts and operations planners to link up with the other organizations in the area; the Special Forces and Rangers also put liaison officers in all of the Stryker brigade meetings.

Colonel Brown pushed mission authority down to company commanders as well as "lower[ing] the level of actionable intelligence" to conduct missions upon best guesses rather than waiting for perfect information. Stryker units were given independent areas of operation for which they were responsible, enabling Soldiers to become very familiar with a particular area. Intelligence collection and targeting decisions were usually done at the battalion and lower echelons; indeed, the bulk of important operational decisions may have been made at the squad and team level.[82] The brigade also developed and used tactical human intelligence teams that would go on missions to interrogate suspects, thus enabling the intelligence-operations fusion so familiar to the brigade's staff officers with Special Operations experience.[83] This increased the number of self-initiated missions and amount of actionable intelligence generated by operations, which in turn led to more missions. Soldiers learned they had to hit a target within 45 minutes of receiving a tip in order to be successful; armed with the new tactics and authorities, they could accomplish this. A captain might conduct a search or raid that generated new intelligence and, without

Figure 5a.

As security deteriorated in Mosul in 2005, Task Force Freedom began working more closely with other military and interagency partners. Snipers from 1ˢᵗ Brigade, 25ᵗʰ Infantry Division Stryker Brigade Combat Team watch over Iraqi police station in Mosul following insurgent attack.

U.S. Army (Jeremiah Johnson)

the need for permission from higher headquarters, immediately hit new targets.[84] The advanced communications architecture and decentralized leadership model made it possible to rapidly redirect units in response to new information and "swarm" the enemy by having nearby units quickly surround the insurgents.[85] The Intelligence Community was eager to work closely with Task Force Freedom because it was using intelligence to go on the offensive. The brigade began using unique intelligence assets for massed electronic and human monitoring of the enemy, exploring techniques that would become known as "network targeting." SOF and conventional forces worked together to put "persistent pressure" on a terrorist network until it collapsed. The terrorist networks inside Mosul were also in the process of being physically isolated from the outside world by means of a long berm around the city and a series of checkpoints that controlled movement into the city.[86]

By late March 2005, Colonel Brown was able to note two measures of success in Mosul. First, calls to the tip hotline on insurgent activity increased tenfold, from 40 a month in late 2004 to 400 a month in early 2005. Second, captured al Qaeda leaders reported that 80 percent of al Qaeda's networks around Mosul had been destroyed.[87] Even better, in April, Task Force Freedom received a major boost when Major General David Rodriguez took

Figure 5b.

In Mosul, Iraqi police officer monitors detainee following raid that captured three terrorists, including a high-ranking al Qaeda official.

U.S. Air Force (Jeremy T. Lock)

command of it and Multinational Force–Northwest. The expansion of Task Force Freedom brought the extra military and civilian assets available to a 2-star division commander;[88] almost 200 additional staff[89] as well as more "gunslingers" in the form of the 3d Armored Cavalry Regiment, which took control of the area to the north and west of Mosul, extending to the Syrian border, in April and May 2005 (see figure 6). Rodriguez also brought extra "force of personality" in support of a flatter organization, a whole-of-government approach to counterinsurgency, and a determination to take the fight to the jihadis at every level and with all means available. He broke down organizational barriers, cajoling personnel from other departments and agencies and then meeting their personnel to make sure they knew they were important and valued members of Task Force Freedom. Rodriguez's rule was "no secrets": all liaison officers saw and participated in staff products. For example, Rodriguez added another weekly coordinating discussion that his chief of staff

Figure 6.

Heavy fighting took place in
Mosul in spring 2005

Michael Yon (used with permission)

led but that he and his deputy attended. During this meeting, Task Force Freedom and its partners would decide on targeting, how best to use intelligence, surveillance, and reconnaissance (ISR) assets and financial and engineering resources, and which reconstruction projects to support.

Task Force Freedom was successful. A study by RAND reported that it "succeeded in protecting the civilian populace more effectively in Mosul than elsewhere in the country—even after the enemy had chosen to make targeting cooperating Iraqi civilians a 'center of gravity' in the conflict."[90] Desperate Mosul insurgents were reduced to using alcoholics and mentally ill patients for suicide attacks. Task Force Freedom's success was based on organizational improvements that allowed the free flow of information: "What we tried to do was break down the walls, make sure there's no stovepipe and make sure that everybody has access to things. The intent is . . . from National, down to the foot Soldier on the ground, that these guys have access to the best information and it's timely, relevant, accurate, and actionable."[91] An in-depth analysis from the Joint Center for Operational Analysis explains the conditions necessary for the free flow of information within the task force and also its net effect:

The dynamic that made this all work was the personal involvement of individuals from each agency and their dedication to serving the task force and its mission, rather than their parent organizations. New levels of interagency trust and combat-necessity gave birth to an unprecedented innovation: a national level intelligence team in direct support of a tactical task force.[92]

Task Force Freedom's organizational innovations were linked with its population-centric counterinsurgency strategy. Rodriguez considered money a weapon, to be used in projects that would win popular support and improve security.[93] The task force thus "chipped away at the iceberg" of insurgent sympathizers by offering jobs and sanitation programs to Mosul's population and even gifts such as cell phones to the children of former Revolutionary Guards.[94] The task force rebuilt the police force with the help of Department of Justice International Criminal Investigative Training Assistance Program (ICITAP) representatives[95] (despite lukewarm support from higher echelons in Baghdad). They also constructed a building to serve as an intelligence fusion and operations center for Iraqi police, military, medical, and municipal leaders as well as their American advisors. The task force also tasked the conventional forces to conduct more detention, interrogation, and intelligence activities. All these measures greatly increased available human intelligence, which was critical. To effectively target the clandestine cells, the teams had to understand each terrorist's patterns of life and social networks.[96] Eventually, the task force was able to track the flow of foreign fighters back to Syria and thus work with the Border Defense to put pressure on smuggling routes.[97] Task Force Freedom also expanded training for the Iraqi Security Forces, partnering 21 Iraqi battalions with Special Forces A-teams, mostly from the Arabic language–qualified 5th Special Forces Group. Rodriguez had to work hard to have resistance from U.S. Special Operations Command overturned by the Pentagon, but the Special Forces arrived within 5 weeks and did great work with the local Iraqi forces.

While the security situation in Mosul was making a dramatic recovery, Iraq as a whole was becoming less stable. With perhaps as many as 200 foreign fighters entering Baghdad each month in 2006,[98] "sectarian violence in Baghdad was out of control, with AQI [al Qaeda in Iraq] conducting high profile attacks on Shia targets, and Shia Jaysh al Mahdi conducting extrajudicial killings of Sunnis."[99] Based on the successful experience of Mosul, interagency intelligence fusion cells began to spread across Iraq[100] at multiple echelons, from brigade to theater level.[101] They were not all equally successful, however, for reasons that were not immediately apparent.[102] Nevertheless, the new intelligence fusion cells began serving the whole range of interagency and military organizations while Smith's forces maintained their own independent interagency task forces and focused on eliminating senior al Qaeda leaders. The cells provided a place and means for interagency partners to collect and analyze intelligence and to coordinate efforts to eliminate enemy networks,[103] but unlike Smith's interagency task forces, they remained detached from operational units. Thus, coordination between intelligence fusion cells, high-value target teams, and the local conventional commander still required sustained effort. As in Mosul, intelligence fusion cells tended to push their actionable intelligence to the units in their area that proved most able and willing to take action.

The 3ᵈ Armored Cavalry Regiment in Tal Afar

As Task Force Freedom began consolidating its gains, Colonel H.R. McMaster's 3ᵈ Armored Cavalry Regiment (ACR) arrived at Tal Afar, just northwest of Mosul. Like Mosul, Tal Afar had not been protected by an adequately sized U.S. force in 2004—just a single company—and by the spring of 2005, it had fallen under the sway of insurgent forces.[104] The 3ᵈ ACR had been preparing to relieve the 1ˢᵗ SBCT for months. In November 2004, an advance team had arrived to survey the situation just as the Battle of Mosul erupted. Over the next several weeks, they worked with Colonel Brown to develop a transition plan and witnessed the power of Task Force Freedom's organizational innovations, particularly the development of the intelligence fusion cell and partnering with the regional Embassy office. Based on those observations, the 3ᵈ ACR knew it "needed to be tied in with the embassy and the political effort more broadly."[105] However, orders changed, and the 3ᵈ ACR was assigned to Baghdad. It conducted another pre-deployment site survey and again concluded the unit would need to work with a wide range of interagency partners to accomplish its mission.[106] To prepare a whole-of-government solution, they dispatched Lieutenant Colonel Paul Yingling, the "effects coordinator"[107] for the 3ᵈ ACR, to Baghdad several months in advance of their deployment to establish connections with as many interagency partners as he could, particularly the Departments of Agriculture and Justice, USAID, and the Police Reconstitution group.[108]

Upon arriving in Baghdad in April 2005, the 3ᵈ ACR again was redirected, this time to Nineveh Province to gain control over Tal Afar. The regiment would be split between Baghdad and Nineveh until late May but immediately set about creating the conditions for a successful counterinsurgency campaign in Tal Afar.[109] In order to make sense of the city and the various factions that controlled it, the 3ᵈ ACR thoroughly reconnoitered Tal Afar and its surrounding environs. Insurgents in Tal Afar drew support from kinship networks extending into the neighboring villages as well as from the smuggling networks that connected Tal Afar with Syria, a source of money, guns, and foreign fighters. To isolate Tal Afar from these networks, the 3ᵈ

ACR increased border patrols, began using biometric devices at checkpoints, and also worked with the ICITAP group training the Iraqi border defense forces. Training the Iraqi Customs and Border Patrol services was a major challenge because they had been infiltrated by insurgents and aided smugglers and foreign fighters coming to Iraq. Identifying the traitors required a sustained, combined intelligence effort. The 3[d] ACR also obtained support from higher echelons for their efforts, receiving in particular some helpful long-range ISR. McMaster also worked closely with SOF in the area who had access to and influence with the local sheikhs. The U.S. forces shared money and intelligence to influence the sheikhs to assist U.S. efforts to stifle infiltration across the border by the enemy.[110]

During the summer of 2005, the 3[d] ACR also did a thorough analysis of Tal Afar to determine what would be required to rebuild the city after it was pried away from the insurgents. The regimental staff secured Commander's Emergency Response Program money in advance and bought the equipment needed to reestablish the most important services in the aftermath of their attack, including provision of adequate water and electricity. Colonel McMaster worked with representatives from the Department of Justice and from USAID Transition Initiatives to develop contracts for reconstruction, connecting them with the Tal Afar city council and providing military staff officers to assist their work.[111] The regiment also set up tent cities for refugees, detailed civil affairs staff to help restore services, and obtained additional reconstruction money.[112] McMaster established ties with the Embassy in Baghdad as well as the regional State Department headquarters in Mosul, from which he secured an Army Foreign Area Officer to write press releases and take pictures and video of the upcoming battle, which would be matched to a global positioning system to track events in the city. Finally, the 3[d] ACR separated the insurgents in Tal Afar from the surrounding villages by building a berm around the city and establishing checkpoints to control traffic in and out of the city. At checkpoints, Soldiers checked travelers for two forms of identification and performed "tactical questioning" to screen for possible insurgents. They also kept informants on hand to visually identify insurgents. The 3[d] ACR swept the villages around the city for insurgents but left two untouched as safe havens. During the operation, they isolated these towns, took photographs of all the males, and then had informants identify the insurgents overnight for arrest the following day.[113]

After months of preparation, the 3[d] ACR troops moved into the city with great deliberation, supported by U.S. Special Forces, elements of the Iraqi Army 3[d] Division and 2[d] Division, Iraqi Special Forces, and Iraqi and Mosul police units (see figure 7). The national police force, which was controlled by militia members, was soon excluded from the operations. Tal Afar was divided between al Qaeda (with whom the mayor was associated) and Iranian-controlled

U.S. Air Force (Aaron Allmon)

Figure 7.

3ᵈ Armored Cavalry Regiment Soldiers conduct combat patrol in Tal Afar

Shia militias (with whom the police chief was associated). The main focus of the assault was an al Qaeda safe haven in the eastern part of the city that had large training facilities, significant amounts of equipment, and good satellite uplinks. As the al Qaeda operatives tried to escape into the western part of the city, coalition forces removed all residents in the area, wrapped three lines of concertina wire around the al Qaeda stronghold, and jammed their communications. This forced them to meet in groups in the narrow alleyways of the city, where they could be easily targeted by Apache helicopters. American and Iraqi soldiers then assaulted and reclaimed the district. In each house, they left a letter written in Arabic explaining the need for the assault and provided compensation for damage. During the operation, between 200 and 300 insurgents were killed and over 500 captured.

After operations to retake the city, the coalition immediately began rebuilding the Tal Afar police force. Money had already been secured to pay the police for their first 45 days in uniform, and the day after the assault, ground was broken on new police stations. The police were formed by precinct and partnered with an Iraqi army unit. The 3ᵈ ACR also set up 29 outposts where U.S. and Iraqi soldiers and local police lived and worked together.[114] The outposts gave the city a strong but diplomatic American presence and allowed McMaster to forge close ties with the city government and the Iraqi commander responsible for the region. The 3ᵈ ACR also worked with the 9 Special Forces A-teams in the area to put the Iraqi soldiers through a comprehensive noncommissioned officer and officer school. Civil Affairs personnel helped reconstitute the city council and strengthen good governance. They took over regimental funds to rebuild the cities and pay workers. Getting the highly visible traffic cops back on the streets and bringing in school teachers to coincide with the opening of new schools were important milestones. However, promoting good governance also required cleaning up the city government. McMaster worked with the provincial governor to remove the mayor of Tal Afar and found another job for the police chief. The Nineveh police chief became Tal Afar's police chief and then its mayor; an apolitical Sunni was found to replace him as the police chief.

Proper coordination with SOF was another important issue. McMaster, who knew the SOF Task Force commander in Mosul, sent a liaison officer to work with him. In return, the task force sent a high-value target team to Tal Afar to support the operation for 2 months and occasionally to conduct supporting operations thereafter. The attitude of the SOF Task Force leader determined the extent of interaction, however, and the arrival of a new leader could result in less communication and cooperation. During one such lull in cooperation, the SOF Task Force unilaterally took out targets "when we had patrol bases nearby and could have just walked to their house."[115] It took an unfortunate incident in which the high-value target team took casualties to impress upon them the need to coordinate with McMaster's forces. McMaster believed the 3ᵈ ACR had an effective raiding capability and preferred that the SOF Task Force share intelligence and let the regiment decide how to act upon it. This required "continuous conversations" between both parties. Inside the city, it was found that operations worked best when the SOF Task Force and the 3ᵈ ACR compared intelligence before missions. The 3ᵈ ACR, with its intimate knowledge of the city's geography and sociology and the regiment's many patrol posts, could more easily detain a suspect, interrogate him, and then hand him over to the SOF Task Force. The special capabilities of the SOF Task Force were best used when assaulting remote areas that had good early warning systems, "but it was ultimately their call."[116]

One of McMaster's deputies later explained, "There are two ways to do counterinsurgency. . . . You can come in, cordon off a city, and level it, à la Fallujah. Or you can come in, get to know the city, the culture, establish relationships with the people, and then you can go in and eliminate individuals instead of whole city blocks."[117] In taking this latter approach, the regiment enlisted the aid of as many interagency partners as it could. Most such work had to be done through Task Force Freedom, which had both experience in working with the interagency and a much bigger staff; but sometimes the 3ᵈ ACR could bring interagency partners directly to Tal

Afar or get extra staff from higher echelons (that is, corps headquarters). Unified interagency and allied efforts were anchored in the strong conceptual foundation and long-term planning work for the retaking of Tal Afar. McMaster's forces also had availed themselves of expert advice from the history department at West Point, insights from the 3[d] ACR's previous experience in Iraq, and lessons learned from many other commanders who served in Iraq between the regiment's first and second tours there. McMaster's approach continued the pattern pioneered in Mosul but received far more press attention and became a highly visible model for emulation by other commanders.

1st Brigade Combat Team in Ramadi, Anbar Province

When Colonel Sean MacFarland and his 1st Brigade Combat Team, 1st Armored Division, arrived in Ramadi, Anbar Province, in June 2006, he had successful examples of combined counterterrorism-counterinsurgency tactics to draw upon. He would need them. Ramadi was so dangerous that it had been written off by the senior Marine Corps military intelligence officer as a lost cause;[118] it was experiencing three times more attacks each day, per capita, than any other location in Iraq.[119] Over the next 9 months, however, the reinforced Army–Marine Corps brigade led by Colonel MacFarland would turn Anbar Province into one of the greatest success stories of the American occupation (see figure 8). MacFarland "plagiarized shamelessly" from the successes of previous successful commanders and in the process proved the importance of wedding interagency high-value targeting with sound counterinsurgency principles. From Colonel Michael Shields, whose 172[d] Stryker Brigade had replaced the 1st Stryker Brigade Combat Team in Mosul, MacFarland learned the importance of integrating counterterrorism and counterinsurgency operations. He immediately exchanged staff with other U.S. forces in the area to build a common picture of the enemy networks. He wanted to eliminate "source fratricide" and target enemy leaders to reduce pressure on the populace while he worked to secure their safety and allegiance.[120] From McMaster, he took the need to establish combat outposts to protect the population and engage local leaders to win their support. Drawing on his own experience in Bosnia, where he had seen the importance of training and equipping locals, he decided to build up the local Iraqi security forces. MacFarland pursued a strategy "centered on attacking Al-Qaeda's safe havens and establishing a lasting presence there to directly challenge the insurgents' dominance of the city, disrupting their operations, attriting their numbers, and gaining the confidence of the people."[121]

The assets at MacFarland's disposal to execute his strategy differed from those available in Mosul. His brigade had much less organic intelligence architecture, lacking the electronic hardware and software of Stryker units. MacFarland also had significantly fewer interagency re-

Figure 8.

COL Sean MacFarland (second from left)
is briefed on mortar attack in Ramadi

U.S. Air Force (Jeremy T. Lock)

sources in his area of operations, due partly to interagency personnel shortages and the absence of infrastructure that could be exploited with non–military intelligence capabilities. On the other hand, the reduced interagency presence meant he only had to engineer the cooperation of the Intelligence Community, the Special Forces teams who were part of the Combined Joint Special Operations Task Force–Arabian Peninsula, and elements of Smith's Task Force targeting al Qaeda leadership in the area. There were initial coordination problems. For example, SOF Task Force units would slap down large restricted operational zones (ROZs) over the city whenever they conducted a takedown, interfering with MacFarland's ability to provide fire support to his units. This allowed the insurgents to attack MacFarland's Soldiers from the rooftops with relative impunity.

Within the space of a month, however, cooperation between the Intelligence Community, SOF, and MacFarland's brigade improved. The brigade staff and SOF Task Force personnel in particular exchanged targeting files and prisoners and sat in on each others' targeting meetings, eventually leading to a "seamless targeting process through liaison officers and the fusion center." Collaboration was enhanced by collocation and a shared culture. The brigade and the SOF Task Force units were located on the same forward operating base, and MacFarland's deputy commander and one of his battalion commanders had worked in Special Operations before, so they "knew the secret handshake." General Smith also came to Ramadi several times to meet with MacFarland in order to find out how he could help and ensure sufficiently high levels of cooperation. Most importantly, MacFarland was able to forge a common understanding of the mission: making Ramadi safe.[122]

Integrating operations set the stage for success. Smith's forces began using "mini ROZs" when conducting raids, allowing the conventional forces to conduct simultaneous operations and receive supporting fires. Although the special operators initially worried that cooperating with conventional forces would slow down their operations, it did the opposite. Brigade forces "flushed" insurgents "like a nest of quail, and the [SOF Task Force] would be in a good position to pick off their . . . targets."[123] The brigade also benefited from cooperation with SOF. Al Qaeda brutally attacked any tribe around Ramadi inclined to support the coalition.[124] By taking out terrorists, the SOF Task Force "scared the bejeebers out of them" and provided a "critical enabler that gave the tribes breathing space."[125]

After Smith's forces killed or captured high-value targets, MacFarland sometimes had an opportunity to "flip" the Sunni tribes to actively support his troops. His units would then set up combat outposts in the tribal territory to provide them with security, recruit police and auxiliaries from among the Iraqis, and make friends through "goat grabs" and other efforts to win their respect and cooperation. Previous units operated from forward operating bases outside the city, driving in on patrols to exchange gunfire and then retreating, but MacFarland set up outposts in the city where U.S. Soldiers and Iraqi police lived and worked together, maintaining a continuous presence.[126] The local militia proved loyal even under extreme duress. After one police station was completely destroyed by an al Qaeda bomb, the survivors insisted on returning to patrol their neighborhood that afternoon to send the message that they would not be intimidated.[127] These tactics, combined with improved local intelligence gained through their new allies, forced high-value targets to move to areas controlled by other tribes. When al Qaeda operatives moved to a new area, the tribe in that area would request protection from the Americans, starting the cycle over again.

These cooperative tactics produced a bellwether moment. Al Qaeda launched a punitive attack against a tribe that was considering support for the coalition, and tribal leaders called U.S. forces to ask for support. MacFarland's men could not reach them in time, but they convinced the SOF Task Force to immediately divert an armed Predator unmanned aerial vehicle to the scene. The Predator caught the al Qaeda men in their pickups, dragging the bodies of slain tribesmen behind them—a sign of gross disrespect for their Muslim coreligionists. The

Predator destroyed the pickups with its Hellfire missiles, and the impressed tribe aligned itself with the coalition. Others soon followed.[128] According to MacFarland, this incident and others illustrated the strategic impact of having the SOF Task Force in direct support of conventional forces conducting counterinsurgency operations.[129]

The "Anbar Awakening" has been characterized as a simple case of buying the temporary loyalty of the Iraqi militias, but participants scoff at this explanation. One officer recalled, "We had to prove to them that we were worthy allies; America's track record as an ally? Pretty spotty. . . . it took a leap of faith to come out and join the U.S."[130] One of MacFarland's major innovations was designed to reassure the undecided tribes. He reversed existing policy, which was to tell the tribes, "You stand up, we stand down." Instead of communicating an intention to leave Iraq to Iraqis, MacFarland expressed commitment to their cause. He explained that if the Iraqis stood up for themselves, he and his forces would stay until they were "secure from al Qaeda and the Persians [Iranians]."[131] He promised to create a Sunni police militia that would become part of the Iraqi government but would stay in Ramadi to protect their homes and families. To do so, MacFarland required "non-standard funding sources" available through interagency contacts. He organized both official police and auxiliary police detachments to protect tribal areas, running the Iraqi recruits through a 1-week training course provided by either Navy SEALs from Combined Joint Special Operations Task Force–Arabian Peninsula or the brigade's artillery detachment.[132] In what MacFarland would later describe as "the game changer," Ramadi's police force increased from 150 to 4,000 in a matter of months. Consequently, intelligence and counterinsurgency capabilities improved, and responsibility for security operations eventually began transitioning to the Iraqis. A Department of State cable from the Provincial Reconstruction Team leader in Anbar helped spread the news in Washington on what MacFarland had accomplished in Ramadi. As a result, more funds poured in, and MacFarland was able to cement his early successes.

Bottom-up Innovation

Task Force Freedom's version of "collaborative warfare" was the earliest and most comprehensive one, perhaps because it was implemented in a major city. Yet the better known subsequent innovations in the smaller towns of Tal Afar and Ramadi also featured collaboration among disparate actors engineered as circumstances warranted but also with attention to what had worked well previously in Mosul (see figure 9). In all three locations, commanders built organizations and tactics capable of conducting classic counterinsurgency warfare and demonstrated the insurgency could be beaten. They were able to target the insurgents

Figure 9. Spread of Innovation from Mosul to Tal Afar to Ramadi

and terrorists with sufficient discrimination to put them on the defensive, while population-centric security measures and influence operations pacified the broader population. In retrospect, this kind of collaborative warfare can be characterized as three separate innovations, each of which required interagency collaboration and all of which ultimately had to merge into a unified strategy.

The first innovation was network-based targeting.[133] Characterized narrowly, this meant charting the clandestine terrorist and insurgent cells and their immediate supporters in order to attack them. This approach was formalized as the *F3EA* concept: find, fix, finish, exploit, and analyze (it would later become *F3EAD* with the addition of *disseminate*).[134] F3EAD tactics were critically dependent upon interagency organization and a substantial departure from the Army's more typical D3A (decide, detect, deliver, assess) doctrine, "an artillery bullets and shrapnel approach."[135] Characterized more broadly, network-based targeting meant using all-source intelligence to provide situational awareness of the local environment, its social networks, key decisionmakers, and their motivations. With such knowledge, commanders could influence the population without lethal measures. In short, effective counterinsurgency required knowledge of the human terrain (both enemy clandestine cells and the local population), which could only be achieved by collaboration and information exchange among disparate U.S. organizations and local sources.[136]

The second innovation was the fusion of improved all-source intelligence with operational capability. Having intelligence and operations working together in common space and on a sustained basis produced several benefits: persistent surveillance, improved discrimination, and better decisionmaking. The interagency teams made it possible to eliminate the organizational seams between the different coalition actors in Iraq, placing an "unblinking eye" on high-value targets. Previously, the *find* and *fix* efforts would be led by an intelligence organization, the *finish* performed by a SOF unit, and the *exploit* and *analyze* efforts conducted by other organizations or not at all. Passing responsibilities between units and organizations represented an "organizational blink" during which momentum slowed and the target might escape.[137] In June 2006, the SOF Task Force scored a high-profile success using these tactics when it eliminated key terrorist leader Abu Musab al-Zarqawi:

> *The airstrike that killed Zarqawi was only a fraction of the effort to find and accurately target him. The true operational art behind that strike was a multidisciplined intelligence, surveillance, and reconnaissance (ISR) endeavor coupled with agile SOF that patiently laid bare the Zarqawi network and resulted in a find-fix-finish operation. It took more than 600 hours of ISR to track and observe the network that yielded the target. . . . The SOF–ISR combination was effective because it unified operations and airborne collections with all other intelligence disciplines under a single commander.*[138]

This success eliminated a single terrorist, but more broadly this kind of intelligence-operations fusion provided operators with better situational awareness so they could better decide where and how they applied lethal force. Absent persistent surveillance, high-value target raids or strikes were likely to come up empty or be counterproductive. This was true for both the high-value target teams trying to eliminate enemy leaders and the conventional force commanders trying to secure the population. Finally, this fusion improved decisionmaking on the difficult tradeoffs between developing sources and taking down targets. When operators know the value of a source, they can better judge the value of an operation that compromises the source, and they can be more appreciative of the need to collect certain types of intelligence. Similarly, if intelligence analysts understand the operations their analyses support, they can better tailor them for relevance.[139]

The first two innovations benefited both counterterrorist and counterinsurgency forces, and were pioneered top down by General Smith and his Task Force commanders and bottom up by conventional force commanders in Mosul, Tal Afar, and Ramadi. The third innovation was the integration of counterterrorist and counterinsurgency efforts that characterized operations in Mosul, Tal Afar, and Ramadi, and the proliferation of this model. As intelligence fusion cells and high-value target teams proved themselves, they more frequently were located in proximity to an enemy network in order to mirror it and thus increase the speed of analysis and the rate of the targeting cycle.[140] For example, the SOF Task Force that eliminated Zarqawi was composed of several elements, each of which combined multiple military and civilian partners and which could authorize a raid without needing approval from a higher headquarters.[141] This meant that rather than just practicing "decapitation" (the elimination of top enemy leadership), the SOF teams (broadly construed) "ate their way to the top" from the middle ranks or, if they thought a major terrorist operation was in the works, might even attack down the chain toward the foot soldiers to derail the planned event.[142] The interagency high-value target teams were mobile, moving from pacified locales to the next dangerous areas, which allowed their important skills to be used where most needed. In addition to Smith's forces, other SOF units were conducting high-value target raids as well,[143] and doing so increasingly in collaboration with conventional forces working to extend population-centric counterinsurgency principles. As a result, "You had an interagency synergy at Brigade level, an interagency synergy at Division level, you had it at the Corps and Force level. It allowed an integration of civil and military relationships. . . . we were better able to integrate those [organizational] strengths to get results."[144]

The neologism *collaborative warfare* was therefore apt. Networked-based targeting, fusion of intelligence and operations, and counterterrorist-counterinsurgency integration required unprecedented collaboration between diverse departments and agencies and between SOF and conventional forces. Collaborative warfare employed some new tactics and some new technologies, but neither the tactics nor the technologies could have been used to good effect without the new organizations. It can be argued that al Qaeda overplayed its hand with gruesome tactics[145] and that Iraqis made courageous decisions to risk cooperating with the coalition, but disgust with al Qaeda had to be exploited and cooperation with Iraqis coaxed and nurtured. The high-value target teams put terrorist and insurgent cells on the defensive and conventional force commanders partnered with other departments and agencies and SOF to guide the activities of those teams with a broader awareness of their second- and third-order effects.[146] Together, these innovations set the stage for a dramatic reversal of the security situation in Iraq in 2007, which is why so many participants interviewed by the authors and others voiced a common refrain: "We could not have been successful if it had not been for the interagency."[147] Such conviction was not matched, however, by an understanding of the requirements for effective interagency teams.

Key Variables in Interagency High-value Target Team Performance

Given the demonstrated contribution of interagency approaches to counterinsurgency and counterterrorism in Iraq, it is surprising that there are so few studies of their effectiveness. The two government studies available are not comparable and identify different variables. A CIA Lessons Learned Center study concludes that the three most important factors in determining interagency collaboration were "a shared vision of the importance of its task, location in a single space, and the shared experiences of its members."[148] The Joint Center for Operational Analysis looked specifically at the remarkable achievements of Task Force Freedom in Mosul and attributed its success to seven factors:

- a small staff with a high degree of dependence and trust

- direct involvement of strategic assets at the tactical level

- principals with SOF backgrounds

- coordination and collaboration between strategic, operational, and tactical entities

- communication

- the use of "swarm tactics"

- quickly modifiable tactics, techniques, and procedures.[149]

Here we concentrate on understanding the high-value target teams. We began by questioning participants on the variables prescribed by the Project on National Security Reform but also asked for their insights on other variables they considered important. Based on their responses, it became necessary to modify the variables, generally by broadening them or adding new ones. After an extensive review of literature on cross-functional teams,[150] we concluded that we could modify the variables in a manner consistent with both our research on high-value target teams and the literature from organizational studies (see table 2).

Below, we examine 9 of 10 variables often cited in organizational literature as important determinants of cross-functional team success. They are organized in three sets: one at the organizational level, one at the team level, and one at the subteam level.[151] We provide a brief explanation of each variable and then assess its importance in explaining the success or failure of the interagency high-value target teams in Iraq. The exception is the "composition" variable,[152] which we had insufficient data to assess. Descriptions of team experiences were highly consistent, although sources differed in how they assessed the relative importance of some variables.

Purpose

A common understanding of the team's purpose and an unwavering commitment to it are not always achieved but are well recognized as a key ingredient in success.[153] Purpose can be communicated formally through mandates and concrete goals or less formally by whatever authority convenes or leads the team. Because the high-value target teams seldom had a formal mandate, we adopt the more widely used concept of team "purpose."[154] Sometimes, a general purpose and specific goals are distinguishable but mutually supportive, as organizational management theorists Jon Katzenbach and Douglas Smith argue:

> *A team's purpose and specific performance goals have a symbiotic relationship: each depends on the other to stay relevant and vital. The specific performance goals help a team track progress and hold itself accountable; the broader, even nobler aspirations in a team's purpose supply both meaning and emotional energy.*[155]

The experience with interagency high-value target teams in Iraq substantiates both the importance of purpose and the need to constantly assess the goals that will best advance that purpose. Many interviewees and the CIA study previously mentioned underscored the importance of shared purpose (or vision or goals) and acknowledged that without it, team members had a tendency to

Table 2. Variables in High-value Target Teams

	Project on National Security Reform[1]	Current Study/ Literature[2]
Organizational Level	Clear mandates	Purpose[3]
	Authorities	Empowerment[4] (covers authorities and resources)
	Resources	
		Support[5]
Team Level	Size, location, tenure	Structure[6]
		Decisionmaking[7]
	Culture	Culture[8]
	Team training	Learning[9]
		Composition[10]
Individual Level	Rewards	Rewards[11]
		Leadership[12]

[1] Project on National Security Reform, *Forging a New Shield* (Washington, DC: Project on National Security Reform, 2008).

[2] See James Douglas Orton with Christopher J. Lamb, "Interagency National Security Teams: Can Social Science Contribute?" *PRISM* 2, no. 2 (March 2011).

[3] Leslie A. DeChurch and Jessica R. Mesmer-Magnus, "Measuring Shared Team Mental Models: A Meta-Analysis," *Group Dynamics: Theory, Research, and Practice* 14 (2010), 1–14.

[4] S.E. Seibert, S.R. Silver, and W.A. Randolph, "Taking Empowerment to the Next Level: A Multiple-Level Model of Empowerment, Performance, and Satisfaction," *Academy of Management Journal* 47 (2004), 332–349.

[5] D.G. Ancona and H. Bresman, *X-Teams: How to Build Teams that Lead, Innovate, and Succeed* (Boston: Harvard Business School Press, 2007).

[6] C.B. Gibson and J.L. Gibbs, "Unpacking the Concept of Virtuality: The Effects of Geographic Dispersion, Electronic Dependence, Dynamic Structure, and National Identity on Team Innovation," *Administrative Science Quarterly* 51 (2006), 451–495.

[7] John R. Hollenbeck et al., "Multilevel Theory of Team Decision Making: Decision Performance in Teams Incorporating Distributed Expertise," *Journal of Applied Psychology* 80 (1995), 292–316.

[8] P. Christopher Earley and Elaine Mosakowski, "Creating Hybrid Team Cultures: An Empirical Test of Transnational Team Functioning," *Academy of Management Journal* 43 (2000), 26–49.

[9] A. Edmondson, "Psychological Safety and Learning Behavior in Work Teams," *Administrative Science Quarterly* 44 (1999), 350–383.

[10] "Composition" is shaded because we did not have the data to use this variable for analysis. John Mathieu, M. Travis Maynard, Tammy Rapp, and Lucy Gilson, "Team Effectiveness 1997–2007: A Review of Recent Advancements and a Glimpse into the Future," *Journal of Management* 34 (2008), 410–476.

[11] Jacquelyn S. DeMatteo, Lillian T. Eby, and Eric Sundstrom, "Team-based Rewards: Current Empirical Evidence and Directions for Future Research," *Research in Organizational Behavior* 20, 141–183.

[12] Katherine J. Klein, Jonathan C. Ziegert, Andrew P. Knight, and Yan Xiao, "Dynamic Delegation: Shared, Hierarchical, and Deindividualized Leadership in Extreme Action Teams," *Administrative Science Quarterly* 54 (2006), 590–621.

pursue their own organizational objectives. The interagency high-value target teams understood their purpose was to get the enemy leaders, thereby reducing their ability to intimidate and creating room for governance capacity to grow.[156] This strong sense of purpose held the teams together as they debated the best ways to go about achieving their objective. It was no easy matter sorting out when to hit a target, at what cost to intelligence sources, and to what effect for the overall policy. Getting all parties to agree on the relative risks involved in any course of action required a great deal of transparency on sources and methods, which was difficult to achieve. Even when the requisite information-sharing was achieved, deciding on priority targets and timing was still an inherently contentious matter. Participating organizations had well-established and different metrics for success that inclined team members to value different activities.[157] Without a strong commitment to the team's common purpose, allegiance to individual organizational cultures would dominate and foul collaboration. As one of the few in-depth reviews of fusion cells argued, their "foundational ethos" was "the sense of urgency, purpose and commitment to accomplish a mission."[158]

The official mandates that guided the work of the fusion cells and high-value target teams varied and were often unclear or ambiguous. A former Army intelligence officer with extensive experience in Special Operations who served in numerous interagency fusion cells throughout Operations *Enduring Freedom* and *Iraqi Freedom* told us that mandates need to be specific about their purpose and targets since this not only clarifies tasking authority but also conveys approval for action, thus avoiding delays. He added that the mandate should be signed by a three-star general or higher so that mission support would be guaranteed. Mandates should also be written in conjunction with partner agencies to ensure their ability to cooperate.[159] When official mandates did not meet these criteria, as was typically the case with the high-value target teams, informal clarification of the mandate had to suffice.

Interviewees who worked on high-value target teams frequently noted that a sense of common purpose arose informally rather than formally from idiosyncratic factors, including force of circumstances, leadership, and the mystique associated with Special Operations units. The teams operated at the forward edge of battle, knowing that how well they performed was literally a matter of life and death not only for their compatriots but also for their own members who went out to act upon the decisions enabled by the team's work. Thus, as several interviewees and one study noted, the closer one was to the battlefield[160] and "the more immediate the physical threat," the less departmental differences mattered.[161] In this regard, one participant found the mission focus in Iraq particularly intense compared to the early years in Afghanistan, which were almost "laid back" in comparison.[162] Conversely, bureaucratic divisions in comparatively safe areas were more prominent. For example, organizational infighting was more pronounced in the "green zone" in Baghdad where most U.S. organizations had their headquarters,[163] and especially so in headquarters back in the United States.[164] Similarly, after Task Force Freedom successfully pacified Mosul, its common sense of purpose diminished, leading to a resurgence of departmental cultures and retraction of interagency support.[165]

Common purpose, or "mission focus," was also strengthened by seeing the practical effects of one's work. The vast majority of intelligence analysts who deployed in support of interagency teams had never seen their work lead to anything concrete. As one SOF operator emphasized, many were motivated beyond description when they saw their work and advice acted upon with tangible, immediate results.[166] Moreover, the operators who worked with these analysts were the Nation's best. There was a certain "wow factor"[167] in working shoulder to shoulder with them, and gaining their respect was important to many members of the teams. Participants also noted that good interagency team leaders like Smith were able to keep the interagency high-value target teams sharply focused by providing regular and clear direction on priorities that would best support the larger warfighting effort.[168] Many successful SOF Task Force leaders reinforced the growing camaraderie and sense of common purpose by making a point of publicly thanking members for good performance.

Empowerment

Authorities and *resources* are commonly treated in the literature under the broader label of team *empowerment*.[169] Teams and team leaders can exercise varying levels of authority, but to be effective they must have sufficient control over ways and means to accomplish their purpose.[170] Authority can be conferred upon the team in general and the team leader specifically. The interagency high-value target teams typically were led by SOF officers handpicked by General Smith and empowered to speak for him and to take action independently. However, Smith's forces needed assistance from other agencies and conventional forces, and the authority of the team leader to direct civilian team members was severely limited. In practice, departments and agencies were largely unwilling to devolve control of their assets to members of their organization who served on a team and unwilling to subordinate their agents to interagency team leaders, who were generally Defense Department personnel. Team leaders could designate tasks for team members to accomplish, but they had no means of compelling them to carry out these tasks. As one of our interviewees remembered, "It was ask, not task."[171] Team members often had a different set of orders from their own agency, and some interagency team members were specifically told to listen only to their agency heads.[172] Team leaders could (and on occasion did) send home particularly ineffective members, but this threat was used infrequently for fear of alienating the parent organization.[173] Any direct attempt by the team leader to force team members to do anything they did not want to do could easily lead to open revolt or a passive-aggressive compliance and, in either case, a precipitous decline in team effectiveness. As teams became more successful, the willingness of members to cooperate increased. Nevertheless, the team targeting cycle was often slowed by the need to negotiate with other organizations that had different priorities.

To compensate for the lack of official authority, team leaders worked hard to forge a strong sense of purpose and build upon team successes, which increased enthusiasm and cohesion. They also fully exploited their close relationship with General Smith and the network of liaisons he established with other organizations.[174] Indeed, a study by the Naval Postgraduate School[175] concluded that access to the most senior decisionmakers was the most important determinant of success because it allowed the interagency teams to bypass multiple layers of midlevel approval and obtain cooperation that otherwise would not have been forthcoming. Smith believed that establishing and maintaining the interagency relationships had to be a constant preoccupation: "It's an informal process, based on handshakes, and people change at the senior levels or midgrade levels; the power of those handshakes is not recorded. Therefore, you always run the risk of it degrading over time. We thought about writing memorandums of instruction or memorandums of understanding so that we codified it. My fear was, if we codify it, people are scared to sign contracts, so I felt they would sign a contract [agreeing to] much less than they were willing to actually do."[176] The results justified the effort. As one observer noted, Smith asked for help politely but he "came as close to unity of command in the interagency as you can get."[177]

Controlling the resources required to accomplish a mission may seem an inherent characteristic of well-constituted authority. This is so much the case in the private sector that the adequacy of resources for mission accomplishment is often subsumed under "authorities" or "empowerment." However, leaders sometimes will assign missions without relinquishing control of the necessary resources, which obstructs team success.[178] In government, it is much more common to convey "unfunded mandates," so including resource control as an independent variable has merit for interagency teams. However, as it turns out, the primary resource issue for the interagency high-value target teams was getting personnel from other departments and agencies.[179] Otherwise, they enjoyed the vast resources generally accorded the SOF Task Force and the support appropriate for a national priority effort. One team leader recalled, "We were fat with resources."[180] Although the Department of Defense was the largest contributor of resources to the teams and the military supplied team members with room and board, all agencies contributed some level of funding and material to the teams. Interagency teams forged through bottom-up experimentation were not as fortunate. In the case of Task Force Freedom in Mosul, one officer recalled that Baghdad tended to suck resources away from Mosul even though Mosul experienced a proportionately greater overall number of attacks. At times, U.S. Soldiers resorted to "passing the hat around" to collect money to reward informants.[181] It also is worth noting that conventional units had far fewer mobility and ISR assets than Smith's units.[182]

Support

It is generally recognized that even good teams often fail for lack of support from the larger organization or organizations in which they are embedded. The larger organization must value and promote the use of teams,[183] and higher leaders must provide "just enough support"[184] without being overbearing and stifling team freedom. The systemic support for the interagency teams in Iraq began poorly but soon improved thanks to General Smith's efforts. The FBI was an early partner for reasons suggested by Director Robert Mueller: "Combating terrorism is not a matter of applying either military strength or intelligence assets or law enforcement tools. The old dichotomies between law enforcement and intelligence, and between law enforcement and the military, no longer apply. Combating terrorism requires a coordination of all these resources."[185] Yet even when department or agency heads like Mueller agreed on the need for interagency collaboration, it was difficult getting buy-in from their organizations. One high-value target team member, citing the Intelligence Community as an example, said, "Relations between SOF and the Agency at the operational level are in lockstep. . . . As you step up to middle management level there are some areas where information is not always shared. . . . [But at the] top level it is full and open disclosure. So basically it's a middle management issue."[186] Overcoming middle management resistance required recruiting personnel with access to senior leaders. Smith noted early on that the Intelligence Community would "give you young people who want to deploy, that's great, but what happens is . . . he can't call back to talk to the director. He talks pretty far down the chain; it's natural. . . . Plus, he can't sit at the table with us, at the same level of maturity and experience, and argue with the Commander." By adding senior representatives of other organizations to his personal staff, Smith improved interagency support for the deployed interagency teams. His deputy for interagency coordination constantly communicated the value of their combined efforts and the need to cooperate in the field. In the case of the Department of State, the Ambassador who served with Smith became a liaison to embassies around the globe, smoothing the way for collaboration on the interdiction of terrorists moving to Iraq. These indispensable deputies from the interagency ensured continuous, multilevel support to the interagency high-value target teams, and as Smith later noted: "You can't do that with quarterly trips, or semiannual trips."[187]

When General Petraeus and Ambassador Ryan Crocker took charge in Iraq in 2007, the civilian-military coordination mechanisms were surprisingly rudimentary,[188] a situation they were determined to change. Both men had extensive experience in irregular warfare,[189] and "both Ambassador Crocker and GEN Petraeus approached their tasks with the perspective that success would only come with intense and pervasive civil military cooperation."[190] In addition, Petraeus's command guidance emphasized empowering subordinate teams: "Warfare has never been more complex and never has it required more imaginative leadership. Empower subordinates and push decisions, resources, and authorities to the lowest level possible. Provide appropriate right and left limits for our leaders and give them the flexibility to be imaginative and adaptive."[191] General Petraeus and Ambassador Crocker were supported in their efforts to improve interagency cooperation and secure civilian personnel for Iraq by Lieutenant General Doug Lute, the Assistant to the President and Deputy National Security Advisor for Iraq. Lute became an important but unsung hero in his role as the George W. Bush administration's "war czar," responsive to the "incessant, relentless pounding and pestering" of Ambassador Crocker for more civilian support.[192] Lute was able to cajole recalcitrant departments and agencies into lending adequate support to the interagency effort. General Petraeus noted that prior to Lute's appointment, "You'd state these needs and would lay out what was required but there was never anybody at the National Security Council level . . . who could reach out and really lean on people to try to get them to fulfill the obligation."[193] Similarly, Ambassador Crocker noted the indispensable role General Lute played in securing civilian personnel for Iraq's reconstruction. Thus, both on the scene and in Washington, DC, support for the interagency team concept was high in 2007, and the time was ripe for proliferating the types of collaborative warfare pioneered by Smith and the Army's field commanders in Mosul, Tal Afar, and Ramadi.

Structure

The preceding variables address organizational conditions necessary for team effectiveness and often depend upon organizational factors beyond the immediate control of the team. In contrast, team structure, decisionmaking, culture, and learning are all variables more directly controlled by the team itself. Here we construe team structure to include *size, location, tenure,* and *communications.* The location, size, and duration of teams and their members are readily acknowledged as important factors in their success.[194] While the literature notes that virtual teams can work, the advantages of collocation are well documented. For the most part, the core members of interagency teams in Iraq and Afghanistan were collocated, and participants unanimously agreed this was quite important. In one team leader's experience, communication with team members via telephone, secure video teleconferencing, email, or chat room generates only 50 to 60 percent of the information and understanding that collocation provides.[195] Collocation also helped create a team culture through familiarity: "They lived together, worked together, ate chow together, PT'd [did physical training] together."[196]

Organizational theory suggests that teams should be "*just* large enough to do the work"[197] and that smaller is better—typically 8 to 10 members.[198] Team members we interviewed also agreed that smaller teams, usually 8 to 15 people, were more effective and allowed greater cohesion and trust. Team members still had to network with other organizations, however, so a distinction should be made between the core team and the larger network of participating contacts. In that regard, some members of interagency task forces we interviewed indicated that teams could operate effectively with 20 to 30 people working together.

The tenure of team members is more variable, however, both in theory and practice.[199] It is generally accepted that teams benefit from new blood but that new members pass through a phase of lower productivity before reaching higher performance levels. It is also widely agreed that retaining team members too long can reduce team effectiveness if it leads to groupthink that reduces creativity or to member burnout. All team members worked full time, which was essential, and in some cases worked excessively. Team leaders had to guard against people working to the point of exhaustion, and sometimes ordered them to take rest.[200] Many teams tried to develop a schedule for standard products and procedures in a 12-hour cycle, rotating teams on and off for that period of time. In the case of the interagency high-value target teams, member tenure was variable but short by industry standards. Most tours of duty for interagency team members and SOF are 90 to 120 days. Multiple deployments mitigate the turnover problem to some extent, but some agencies preferred to rotate in new people for each tour.[201] Smith favored the expectation of repeat tours to sustain commitment to excellence: "I mean, whether the person's the best person in the world, if you are going somewhere for 6 months or a year, and when you leave you're not going to go back . . . how can you have the same focus?"[202] On the other hand, some observers of the teams felt that performance peaked at three or four deployments, after which complacency tended to trump innovation.[203]

Common communications also made a significant contribution to collaboration. General Smith set up unique systems in supporting agencies to facilitate communication[204] and made the same equipment available to conventional forces where necessary.[205] He made a habit of conducting teleconferences at least weekly to keep all parties informed and to recognize their organization's contributions.[206] In this respect, Smith had some help from the Pentagon.

Secretary of Defense Donald Rumsfeld directed his Under Secretary for Intelligence to "make defense intelligence relevant," which led to the formation of a study team that paved the way for new joint intelligence technologies. Soon it was possible to access multiple forms of intelligence on one terminal.[207] Such a common communication backbone facilitated "reachback" to departments and agencies, which was important for interagency team success. According to one experienced participant, the power of collaboration via a "global chat room" was something to behold.[208] Similarly, Task Force Freedom in Mosul eliminated all firewalls that separated interagency communications and provided classified computer connections to all agencies. The task force also made sure five high-quality Army captains followed flag officers visiting local sheikhs to take notes and ensure that any promises made were followed up on immediately so the United States would be perceived as reliable and coherent.[209] Using shared communications networks and putting computer systems with varying levels of classification in the same room also increased transparency and collaboration. With all the relevant information in the same space and team members free to discuss their issues across all types of intelligence and operational seams, it was possible to build a common understanding of the mission and challenges and of the enemy networks.

Decisionmaking

Although many teams tried to develop a battle rhythm of sorts, decisionmaking on the high-value target teams was apparently quite idiosyncratic, in part due to the dynamic environment and diverse skills of the team members. Describing the decisionmaking process without revealing sensitive tactics, techniques, and procedures is difficult. However, one major decision dynamic repeatedly referenced by interviewees fits nicely with team decisionmaking theory. Decisionmaking in cross-functional teams is rooted in the observation made by James Thompson[210] long ago that some task environments are characterized by "reciprocal interdependence" and require a two-way interrelationship or "mutual adjustment" among team members. Studying strategic bomber wings, he described how the output of one party became input for others:

> *Since the aircraft and its equipment could only be operated effectively by a ten-man team of specialists, and since each had to adjust his actions to the actions of others, the bomb wing ultimately depended on the mutual adjustment of the members of this team. . . . Under crucial conditions, the mutual adjustment of crew activities had to be almost instantaneous; hence communication had to*

be rapid, direct, and unambiguous. Regular operation of the crew as a team permitted individuals to learn each other's idiosyncrasies and action habits, thus facilitating mutual adjustment [emphasis original].[211]

Thompson noted that because there is exchange and sharing between team members, such groups are truly interdependent. Because interrelated groups must communicate their requirements and respond to each other's needs, reciprocal interdependence is the most costly and difficult element to coordinate and requires mutual adjustment or feedback.[212] *Mutual adjustment* captures the basic decisionmaking relationship between the SOF Task Force operators and the other Intelligence Community personnel. There was a constant tension between the desire of the intelligence organizations to develop sources and targets and the desire of Smith's operators to take out targets even at the expense of compromising sources.

The mutual adjustment was intense and immediate. One SOF operator recalls that intelligence analysts had to get used to the notion that they were no longer in the business of producing well-crafted reports for easy reading but rather short and quick inputs to targeting folders. Similarly, SOF had to develop patience as their commanders worked through the advantages and disadvantages of taking down targets or tracking them in hopes of more leads. Decisionmaking had to be interactive and analytic. If either side believed the other was not sensitive to its needs and point of view, the conflict could destroy mutual trust and derail the productivity of the team. Given the limited tasking authority of team leaders, cooperation was fragile, so the best team leaders learned how to co-opt without pushing too hard.[213] Team members had to feel that their input was taken into account and that the final decision about whether to act on any given target was made in the best interests of the larger mission and not with any one organization's perspective or equities in mind.

Culture

Cross-functional teams require a culture that accords legitimacy to the team mission and allows the team members to collaborate while still making the most of their varying perspectives and expertise.[214] One person referred to working in an interagency fusion cell as "the *Star Wars* bar scene"[215] because of the diverse organizations and personnel backgrounds represented. Creating a team culture in such an environment was particularly important. Some agencies, particularly those from the Intelligence Community, were worried about sending people to work in interagency teams, fearing that it would compromise their unique equities and cause team members to value information-sharing above departmental procedure. For example, the culture of one intelligence agency gives precedence to safeguarding sources and protecting agents and access over the long term, well after military operations ramp down. The intelligence analysts who deployed to work with the interagency teams were able to operate beyond the close scrutiny of their normal supervisors, but they still needed to communicate up their chain for support and were assessed for their loyalty to their parent organization. According to one senior intelligence service source, if young analysts in the field with the teams began using the pronoun "we" or explaining what the team leader wanted when making requests for support, their parent headquarters would conclude they had "gone native" and lost their longer term perspective, and then restrict them from the more sensitive intelligence.[216] Other Intelligence Community organizations had a reputation for rigidly protecting their sources and methods and were extremely reluctant to reveal them. Finally, some SOF operators simply could not fathom the way law enforcement organizations gave priority to judicial procedures while in a war zone where Americans were dying.

To overcome such deeply entrenched bureaucratic cultures, military personnel tried to "operationalize the interagency" by having other departments and agencies deploy personnel to the field in Iraq to improve organizational support, thus creating countervailing team cultures based on the intense urgency of the deployed team's immediate experience.[217] The intent was to weaken if not override the parent organization's cultural predilections, not to the singular benefit of the SOF Task Force but to the benefit of their collective enterprise. This was the explicit goal established by General Smith and carefully pursued by his best team leaders. The first culture they had to change was their own. Smith had to convince his subordinates that they could not rely solely on their own capabilities; they needed the cooperation of others. In addition, they would have to trust others beyond their own small teams, and to develop that trust, they would have to become much more transparent.

At Smith's direction, the SOF commanders of the interagency teams worked to create a culture of openness that began first and foremost with sharing their knowledge and assets. All organizations withheld information on occasions, but SOF Task Force personnel were directed to set the example by being first to give more information. They were told to "share until it hurts." As one commander explained it, "If you are sharing information to the degree where you think, 'Holy cow, I am going to go to jail,' then you are in the right area of sharing."[218] The point was to build *trust*, and information-sharing was the icebreaker. Personal trust was also an important factor. SOF Task Force members accorded one another that trust and extended it to other team members as shared experience built a reservoir of mutual respect. Even less capable performers would be treated with respect in hope of short- and long-term benefits to interagency teaming.

The urgency of the deteriorating situation in Iraq and the shared danger and intensity of their common situation also encouraged a culture of collaboration and dedication that built mutual trust over time.

Learning

Team training is a narrow concept that has evolved in the literature as a subset of the broader characteristic of team *learning*.[219] Formal training in skills such as conflict resolution and problem-solving is generally considered important for creating effective teams.[220] Such training is particularly important when the team leader has no explicit authority over other team members, as was true in the case of the high-value target teams. Prior training is also generally considered important when the team is working in a high-stress environment. In this regard, the interagency high-value target teams were ill prepared for their missions. The interagency members received scant training before deploying. One SOF commander complained, "You wouldn't prepare a baseball team for a pro season without going through a farm system and doing spring training. . . . yet, we want to do that. Then we are surprised when we don't play well."[221]

Early on, interagency teams received no training at all. Later, some of the participating organizations developed predeployment training programs, and sometimes individuals took the initiative to introduce themselves to other organizations and personnel before deploying. The best training seems to be done by the FBI, which ensures its agents receive training in military tactics, techniques, and procedures before deployment, as well as specialized training for specific skills such as evidence recovery, bomb disposal, or biometrics. There is also an extended course for members of the hostage rescue team. In addition, FBI agents often spend 1 to 3 weeks prior to deployment training with the military unit they will accompany overseas.[222] The agency most frequently lauded by military personnel for sending their best people ("top-notch professionals"[223]) was the FBI,[224] but we are not sure to what extent their well-regarded performance was a function of their predeployment training.[225] Another organization has a classified 6-month curriculum for teaching interagency collaboration,[226] and elsewhere there is a 3-week staff integration course to prepare newcomers for work in fusion cells.[227]

Similarly, there was little predeployment training in interagency collaboration for the conventional forces. Senior leaders like Generals Smith and Petraeus had a cadre of interagency experts whom they brought along from assignment to assignment[228] as well as their own interagency experience to draw upon—General Smith from his SOF background, and General Petraeus from serving as the Deputy Commander of the U.S. Joint Interagency Counter-Terrorism Task Force in Bosnia created immediately following 9/11.[229] Other officers exploited the knowledge of their more experienced colleagues, sometimes even arranging for ad hoc training. Colonel Pete Bayer, the Task Force Freedom Chief of Staff, is a case in point. Bayer trained his personnel on how to work with interagency partners prior to their deployment to Mosul, which became an important enabler in Task Force Freedom's success.[230] Impressed by then–Major General Peter Chiarelli's work in Baghdad to restore facilities (using the SWEAT model: sewer, water, electricity, and transportation), Colonel Bayer dispatched personnel to water treatment plants, electrical works, police stations, and hospitals to learn how they functioned. Such training better prepared his team to work with Iraqi leaders, the Corps of Engineers, and the Department of State personnel in Mosul.

While there was not much predeployment training for the high-value target teams, there was substantial learning over time. Just as conventional force commanders learned from previous experience in Mosul, and then from Tal Afar and Ramadi, SOF Task Force commanders and their teams learned from experience. The system relied heavily on "repeat offenders," or team members who deployed multiple times. Among SOF leaders, on-the-job experience was widely agreed to be the best training, and there was a competition of sorts to get the right veterans assigned to one's team. Even failed teams provided useful experience. One interviewee recalled that his otherwise disappointing experience on JIATF–Former Regime Elements was a "discovery experience [that] seasoned many of us."[231] As experience, experimentation, and shared insights proliferated, learning occurred. High-value target teams initially focused on simply killing and capturing terrorists on their target lists. As the teams grew more collaborative, they began exchanging liaison officers with the conventional forces in their area of operation, which helped them understand the importance of assessing the second- and third-order effects that conducting raids had on the counterinsurgency effort.[232] By December 2006, they had added public affairs officers to each interagency high-value target team to get their version of events out before the enemy could. They advanced from achieving their own narrow tactical goals that were sometimes detrimental to the overarching strategic goals of the war to being a major enabler of the strategic success of the surge in U.S. forces in 2007.

Rewards

Beyond the direct processes of the team itself and its larger organizational milieu, much team literature is directed at the attributes of the individual team members. We did not have enough data to examine personnel profiles, but we did consider other individual-level variables such as rewards and leadership. It is generally agreed that team members are more effective when they are rewarded for high performance[233] and for their contribution to team success rather than just individual success.[234] SOF Task Force team leaders were conscious of the need to recognize and reward personnel from other departments and agencies. They did so for both short- and long-term reasons. In the short term, calling out a team member for special recognition helped cement loyalty to the team mission, and over the long term it was thought useful for building a network of interagency contacts who knew and appreciated SOF. As General Smith explained with respect to recognizing the performance of interagency partners: "You had to employ them so that everybody that went back said, 'Boy, that was the best experience I ever had. I'm really making a difference.' Two, you needed to constantly show what they were contributing. . . . organizations are like people, when they are reinforced positively, they tend to repeat the behavior."[235]

Public praise within the team was perhaps the most important and certainly the most immediate reward, but as the teams became better established, many SOF Task Force leaders made sure they turned out a steady stream of letters of commendation and Department of Defense awards and medals for team members. Successful teams also received unit citations for high performance.

Leadership

General Smith believed selecting appropriate team leaders was critically important to a high-performance interagency team, and our interviewees and the literature on team performance[236] agree with him. Studies suggest personal attributes such as the ability to work collaboratively, a sense of personal empowerment and ability to affect outcomes, and a willingness to stay open to new information and adapt to a dynamic environment positively relate to team performance.[237] Smith recognized the need for special leadership early, handpicking the people he wanted to head his interagency teams. SOF Task Force personnel are extremely task-oriented, but General Smith was looking for those "triple-A-plus people who could switch to a type-B personality in a heartbeat."[238] It was important that his team leaders be able to discuss and cajole rather than simply demand their preferred solution while still retaining a strong sense of urgency. Recognizing this, General Smith chose individual team leaders carefully to maximize the chances that they would succeed in building a culture of collaboration. Doing so was particularly important given the limited authority team leaders had to task other team members.

Interagency High-value Target Teams During and After the Surge

"Collaborative warfare" was ready to go mainstream when the Petraeus-Crocker team arrived in 2007 bringing a coherent counterinsurgency strategy and whole-of-government approach to operations in Iraq. The Task Force Freedom experience in Mosul was not widely appreciated, perhaps because al Qaeda later made a resurgence there. However, the experience in Tal Afar influenced

Washington's view of counterinsurgency strategy, and General Petraeus in particular recognized the importance of what had happened in Ramadi.[239] Petraeus and Crocker provided comprehensive support for interagency solutions, including a jointly signed campaign plan for Iraq.[240] They were able to get more civilian personnel deployed for interagency teams and encouraged "a more widespread understanding of network targeting principles . . . and the 'pushing down' of authorities and resources."[241] Interagency targeting teams proliferated, as did interagency fusion cells in general. The surge of five additional Army brigades in and around Baghdad, and the increasing numbers of Iraqi conventional forces spreading out among the population to provide them with greater security, enabled the coalition to fully exploit the work of the high-value target teams and their ability to put terrorist and insurgent forces on the defensive (see figures 10 and 11).

By 2007, the interagency high-value target teams were a high-volume, awe-inspiring machine that had to be carefully directed. Petraeus understood this and was up to the task.[242] Between February and August 2007, over 7,000 militia members were detained in Baghdad, and according to one source, British SOF alone were responsible for killing or capturing 3,500 insurgents in Baghdad between 2006 and 2008.[243] Other sources suggest that by 2008, the interagency teams were more discriminating. The Chairman of the Joint Chiefs of Staff lauded their successes, stating that they produced actionable intelligence that led to 10 to 20 captures a night in Iraq.[244] Between June and September 2008, 10 major al Qaeda leaders in Baghdad were captured, mostly by an interagency high-value target team that included representatives from the CIA, FBI, Treasury Department, NSA, National Geospatial-Intelligence Agency, and SOF.[245]

Numbers alone were no indicator of success, however. Building on lessons from Mosul to Ramadi, the high-value counterterrorist targeting had to be tightly integrated into the larger counterinsurgency strategy.[246] As a former executive officer for Multinational Division North–Iraq noted:

What we learned in 2007–2008 is that it was impossible to destroy a terrorist network . . . with pinpoint strikes. You can never get enough of them. . . . But when you put conventional forces in those areas and you deny the enemy the safe haven that he enjoyed, it forces the terrorists to move and communicate, allowing them to be found.[247]

Another officer noted:

We have to attack the threat from different lines of operation; the diplomatic, the political, the rule of law, and the security line operation. . . . to truly be effective,

Figure 10. Declining al Qaeda Influence in Iraq, 2006–2007

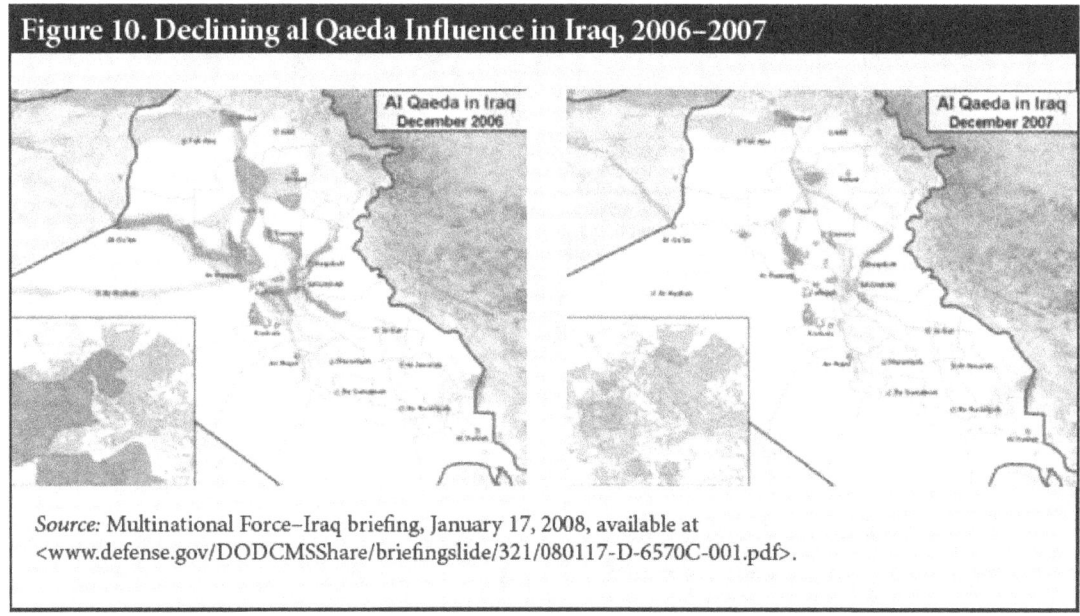

Source: Multinational Force–Iraq briefing, January 17, 2008, available at <www.defense.gov/DODCMSShare/briefingslide/321/080117-D-6570C-001.pdf>.

we have to synchronize those efforts with the killing. If you don't set the conditions to prevent the next guy from standing up, next week you'll be killing a whole different set of individuals but it'll be the same basic positions.[248]

Yet another officer offered a weed metaphor: "It's okay cutting off the foliage, what's above the ground, but unless you get at the roots, it'll just continue growing. . . . that's why it's an effort from across all lines of operation, all elements of national power."[249] These sentiments were deeply held convictions not only for many conventional force commanders by 2007–2008, but also for many SOF commanders who learned it was better not to conduct an improperly coordinated operation because it would do more harm than good. Sometimes this meant scaling back their activities so that one religious or tribal group or another would not feel that it was being unfairly targeted, which would lead to wider resistance.[250]

As security improved during 2007–2008, police and law enforcement tactics came to the fore.[251] The practice of obtaining warrants from Iraqi courts before taking out targets was becoming more widespread by 2007. Evidence needed to be collected so that targets could be captured, brought to Iraqi courts, and put into prison. Otherwise, the length of time that terrorists were detained gave them just long enough to get rested and up to speed on the latest tactics and techniques from their fellow terrorists in detention before being put back on the streets again.[252] Although this necessitated a more thorough and sensitive intelligence-gathering effort,

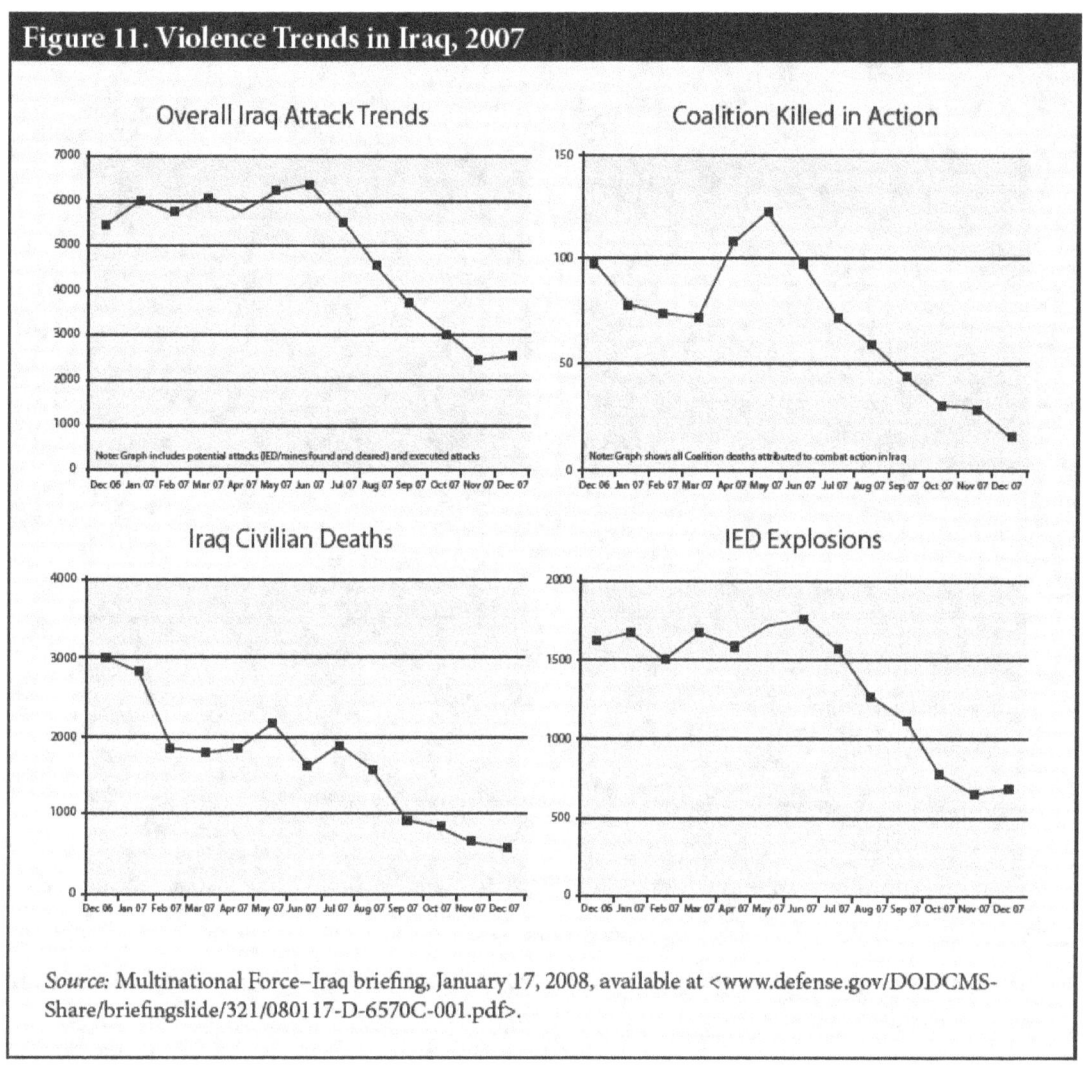

Figure 11. Violence Trends in Iraq, 2007

Source: Multinational Force–Iraq briefing, January 17, 2008, available at <www.defense.gov/DODCMS-Share/briefingslide/321/080117-D-6570C-001.pdf>.

it advanced the network-based targeting trend as intelligence fusion cells began refining the law enforcement–type approach to their work that was used in Mosul in 2005, including specialized software obtained from the law enforcement community that was adapted to analyze insurgent networks.[253] Now the F3EA paradigm changed from find, fix, finish, exploit, and analyze to a more police-like "investigate, arrest, convict, and conduct information operations and statistical tracking of Iraqi officials, witnesses, and conviction rates."[254] A Brigade Combat Team leader explained that:

> *Targeting here in Baghdad is like targeting the mob. There are plenty of guys filling different roles within the networks, and there are always personnel who can step up to*

fill a vacancy. . . . This operation is all about police/detective work. The BCT [brigade combat team] *is not in a rush to force collection and roll-ups. They will continue to track HVIs* [high-value individuals] *and "let it sort out while we collect."* [255]

As predicted in counterinsurgency theory, as security improved, the police and law enforcement agencies began to play a larger role and the interagency teams adjusted accordingly. Intelligence fusion cells increasingly focused on nonlethal targeting. SOF Task Force units that had become much less aloof and more willing to share information with conventional commanders and other agencies[256] also became much more sensitive to the damage that could be done when raids went bad or caused important sections of Iraqi society to become alienated from the American effort. From a counterinsurgency perspective, these developments were positive. Ironically, the collective successes in improving security conditions also presaged the decline of the interagency teams.

Decline and Atrophy

As security improved and Iraqi security forces took a more active role, including joining the interagency intelligence fusion cells for the first time,[257] the overall importance and performance of the interagency teams declined (see figure 12).[258] Several factors explain this deterioration, but the most important one was the growing success of U.S. operations. Initially, everyone understood that the foreign fighters were the target, but some questioned the continuing need for the teams after this threat was largely neutralized.[259] As wider counterinsurgency efforts succeeded and the security situation improved, the sense of urgency declined and along with it the common purpose that was such a driving factor in the success of the teams. Soon, key agencies were reconsidering and consciously lowering their level of commitment. Over the course of the wars in Iraq and Afghanistan, the intelligence agencies had set aside what they considered legitimate concerns about protecting relationships over the long term, doing their primary job of providing objective, detached information to support senior decisionmakers, and ensuring information was not used for inappropriate purposes (that is, for military targeting). After 9/11, there was a powerful incentive and political consensus on the need for "actionable" intelligence against the terrorists, a consensus that inclined the Intelligence Community to lean forward and join the interagency effort to eliminate the terrorist threat by providing analysts for the interagency teams. Once the war effort in Iraq turned around, their organizational focus returned to traditional priorities.[260] In short, as soon as the near-failure in Iraq was averted, bureaucratic support for interagency teams began to decline.

Figure 12.

U.S. Navy (Michael B.W. Watkins)

U.S. forces demonstrate entry tactics for counterterrorism force comprised of coalition and Iraqi forces in Baghdad

By 2008, other departments and agencies, particularly one unidentified intelligence agency, began pulling back people and cooperation, believing information-sharing and collaboration had gone too far.

The gradual withdrawal of interagency support also was inadvertently stimulated by over-exposure and decentralization of SOF liaisons. So many people were claiming to represent Smith's task force that their credibility and clarity diminished.[261] U.S. Special Operations Command also pushed the interagency team phenomenon forward but with so many SOF liaisons in Washington, their purpose and objectives became confusing. Efforts were made to correct the problem,[262] but most agree that by this time "fusion fatigue" had set in. Organizations did not pull their support completely, but instead sent fewer and less experienced personnel. The best personnel were exhausted and returned home or deployed for other purposes. In addition, Smith's departure in June 2008 disrupted relationships that he had personally engineered, making interagency coordination more fragile.[263] At the same time, conventional forces had integrated interagency elements into their own headquarters staffs; human intelligence, cryptologic, and geospatial support teams from various civilian agencies now sat in at brigade headquarters to improve intelligence support.[264] All of these developments allowed and inclined the SOF Task

Force to increasingly focus on Afghanistan, where interagency targeting teams concentrated on collaboration with the SOF Task Force units.[265] More recently, however, intelligence fusion cells and SOF Task Force units appear to be starting to coordinate with nearby conventional forces.[266] In sum, the powerful interagency teams, so dependent upon a shared sense of purpose and commitment, were fueled by circumstances and extraordinary leadership efforts from the SOF Task Force. When circumstances changed and the interagency began withdrawing their support, SOF increasingly turned their focus back to Afghanistan, and the interagency high-value target teams began to atrophy.

Observations

The U.S. experience with interagency high-value target teams justifies several observations. First, organization matters. The interagency teams made a major contribution to reversing the deteriorating situation in Iraq. Interagency teaming was essential to the success of population-centric counterinsurgency efforts pioneered in Mosul and then applied more broadly by Petraeus and Crocker. Interagency teams also took counterterrorism efforts (leadership targeting) to an unprecedented level of efficacy. At the tactical level, the high-value target teams indisputably were transformed by interagency participation. When working well, these teams were able to track their targets and exploit their capture with astonishing speed, permitting great pressure to be applied to enemy leadership and clandestine cells. It also can be argued they made a strategic impact as well: "This speed with which they can turn a piece of information into a target and then engage that target is simply incredible. It has shaped the entire battlefield. It has established the conditions that we now have to conduct these non-kinetic operations to be decisive. That is absolutely a best practice."[267]

At issue is whether the interagency high-value target teams made a strategic impact before or only after they were put to work in support of counterinsurgency objectives. Prior to experimentation in Mosul that married conventional forces and SOF with other department and agency partners, the high-value target teams were not making a strategic impact, and the good they did accomplish was partially offset by collateral damage. After the high-value target teams began cooperating with counterinsurgency forces and paying greater attention to the second- and third-order effects, all the sources we reviewed agreed they were a critical catalyst for success. We do not have the data to weigh the impact of the teams against all other variables that contributed to turning the security situation around or to argue whether other methods could have been used that would have produced less collateral damage. We do believe it is clear, however, that the many new technologies used during the war were less important than the organizational means for bringing all that capability together in an orchestrated effort. We also think it is indisputable that the interagency teams were an incredibly powerful addition to America's irregular warfare arsenal. Both the interagency high-value target teams and the interagency approach eventually embraced by conventional forces demonstrate that how the national security system organizes for complex missions matters greatly.

A second observation is that the interagency teams and the innovations they pioneered are not well understood or respected. Their success often is ascribed to good leadership or to the tremendous capability resident in the SOF Task Force. President Bush acknowledged the success of the high-value target teams by noting that Smith's forces were "awesome."[268] They were, but the SOF Task Force members, studies, and other sources we interviewed unanimously agreed "the interagency" was the key to success. More specifically, network-based targeting, the fusion of multiple lines of intelligence with operations, and the widespread integration of counterinsurgency strategy with highly selective and effective counterterrorist tactics warfare in counterinsurgency—all enabled by interagency teams—made the difference. These innovations are noted in part by some SOF leaders and practitioners,[269] but otherwise are not extolled in the literature and certainly not codified in military doctrine as best practices. Interagency teams are even less appreciated in the broader national security system and beyond. This is regrettable. The interagency teams were a big part of the success in Iraq and need to be appreciated for the role they played in that conflict and for their potential for contributing to the resolution of other complex security problems.

More importantly, the teams deserve sustained attention and study because they were not immediately or consistently effective, and the reasons for the performance variations are not immediately apparent. Some interagency teams simply did not work and had to be abandoned. One such team based in the United States was described as a bus with 15 drivers, each of whom had a foot on the brake and none of whom could depress the gas pedal. In Iraq, some interagency teams, such as the interagency energy fusion cell charged with rebuilding the energy sector, reportedly performed well, while others did not. For the interagency high-value target teams, there was a long learning curve, stretching back to the beginning of the war on terror in Afghanistan. While interagency collaboration provided immediate benefits, the high-value target teams did not hit their stride until 4 years later, between 2005 and 2007. After years of experimentation and experience, some performed better than others, and even successful teams were prone to breakdown. They were "incredibly fragile," in the words of more than one SOF Task Force leader, subject to periodic downturns in productivity if relations among members soured.[270] The variation in the performance of different teams (and in the performance of the same teams at different times) underscores the need to better understand the prerequisites for successful teams so the United States can more consistently exploit their potential.

The third observation from this research is that a more disciplined approach to evaluating the performance of interagency teams is needed. This means greater attention to data collection and a multidisciplinary approach to analysis. Unfortunately, none of the participating organizations (with the possible exception of the chronically overworked National Security Council staff) have any institutional interest in such research. Even in the Department of Defense, there is no effort to track which personnel benefited from experience on interagency teams or led them well. Personnel who now have bureaucratic black belts in interagency collaboration in the field are moving on with their careers in their parent organizations. In addition, the admirable Army oral history databases provide scant insights on performance of the interagency teams because they lack a multidisciplinary perspective. Those conducting the interviews focus on tactical and not organizational insights. One bright note in this regard is the recent creation of the Colonel Arthur D. Simons Center for the Study of Interagency Cooperation at Fort Leavenworth, which may evolve to support sustained and theoretically informed data collection.

It is axiomatic that generalization from a single case study is not possible. However, we paid attention to the way different variables affected team performance in order to begin the process of building a knowledge base for comparative evaluation. The qualitative assessments offered by personnel with direct experience on the teams unanimously attribute greater significance to several of the variables we examined—in particular, common purpose, clearly delegated authorities, small size and collocation, and a supportive organizational context. Teams that did not develop a sense of common purpose were not able to override interference from parent organizations and develop a culture that fostered collaboration. It is also important to note that initially, interagency teams did not benefit from clearly delegated authorities, and performance suffered as a result. Later, in Iraq, the teams were clearly empowered by Smith but this authority did not extend past his task force. Smith decided to forego formal agreements on authorities and rely on the moxie of his officers. History proved him right, but the ambiguity of team and team leader authorities was a constant source of tension and a major reason for the fragility of the teams' performance. Intelligence fusion cells were even less empowered since they lacked an action arm. They had to market products and develop relations with units that were willing, able, and ready to take the offensive against the enemy.

The ability of the teams to learn was critically important. For example, by expanding their range of collaboration to include conventional forces, the SOF Task Force learned to better assess the second- and third-order effects of their operations and make a greater strategic contribution. Finally, broader national security system support for the teams was also an important determinant of their effectiveness. Departments and agencies could hamstring team performance by withholding their support. Nor were teams whose members lacked organizational "reachback" very effective. Consequently, the cooperation of parent organizations could not be taken for granted but instead had to be actively and doggedly pursued by senior leaders in Iraq, the SOF Task Force, and senior leaders in Washington. Cajoling parent organizations for support was a major preoccupation of senior leaders in Iraq.

Conclusion

The interagency high-value target teams in Iraq have attracted surprisingly little attention and study—in effect serving as a "secret weapon" in the fight against terrorism. Bob Woodward's *60 Minutes* exposé on a new operational capability in Iraq doing so much to turn the war around was widely misinterpreted as referring to a magical technology of some sort.[271] But as one interviewee noted, "It wasn't magic; it was collaboration."[272] Collaborative warfare required collaborative organizations. It meant in practice going beyond "jointness" to intense give and take (or *mutual adjustment*) between otherwise disparate military and nonmilitary organizational elements. On the interagency high-value target teams, the collaboration was between the SOF Task Force and diverse intelligence organizations. On the conventional force command staffs, the collaboration was between conventional forces, SOF, and other departments and agencies and Iraqi government entities. When the high-value target teams and integrated conventional force commands collaborated tactically, they produced quick and powerful results. When Petraeus and Crocker used collaborative warfare more broadly in pursuit of a consistent counterinsurgency strategy, the situation in Iraq turned around dramatically. Collaborative organizations are not only powerful but also cost effective. In comparison with new weapons or reconstruction funding, interagency teams cost next to nothing and can be used almost anywhere. However, collaboration is a difficult force to harness and institutionalize. It is not just a function of good leadership, as is often assumed. On the contrary, and as one interagency veteran we interviewed said, organizations that want a reliable record of success do not rely on personalities to generate unity of effort.[273] Neither should the national security system.

Notes

[1] The Joint Center for Operational Analysis (JCOA), meeting notes, author visit, December 8–9, 2010. The authors wish to thank Al Musgrove for arranging the visit and acknowledge the stellar support provided by center personnel informally and through their published products, and in particular Jeanne Burington and Larry Lewis, who led the team that wrote *The Comprehensive Approach: An Iraq Case Study* (Norfolk, VA: JCOA, October 2009), and Robert Hulslander, who authored a separate article on Task Force Freedom.

[2] LTG Raymond Odierno, "The Surge in Iraq: One Year Later," lecture at The Heritage Foundation, March 13, 2008, available at <www.heritage.org/Research/Lecture/The-Surge-in-Iraq-One-Year-Later>.

[3] Scott Simon, "Evaluating the Surge in Iraq," transcript of interview with Stephen Biddle, National Public Radio, September 13, 2008, available at <www.npr.org/templates/story/story.php?storyId=94591166>.

[4] In *The Gamble* (New York: Penguin Press, 2009), Thomas Ricks stresses that changes in U.S. leadership and strategy led to success in Iraq. David Kilcullen, author of *The Accidental Guerrilla* (New York: Oxford University Press, 2009), suggests that the support of the Iraqi population and tribes turned around Iraq. Stephen Biddle emphasized "local, voluntary decisions to stop fighting" in his testimony to the Senate Committee on Foreign Relations, available at <www.cfr.org/publication/15925/prepared_testimony_before_the_senate_committee_on_foreign_relations.html?breadcrumb=%2Fbios%2F2603%2Fstephen_biddle>. In "The Anbar Awakening: An Alliance of Incentives" (*The Washington Quarterly*, January 2009), John McCary argues Iraqi tribal leaders decided to cooperate with the American military out of fear that their positions were being undermined by violence. Others suggest that the United States "bought" stability by paying Iraqi tribesmen; see, for example, Shane Bauer, "The Sheikh Down," *Mother Jones* (September 2009), available at <http://motherjones.com/politics/2009/09/sheik-down?page=2>. Still others argue for a combination of factors; see, for example, Dylan Matthews and Ezra Klein, "How Important was the Surge?" *The American Prospect*, July 28, 2008, available at <www.prospect.org/cs/articles?article=how_important_was_the_surge>.

[5] Bob Woodward, *The War Within: A Secret White House History, 2006–2008* (New York: Simon and Schuster, 2008), 380. The JCOA is another major source, albeit one within the government, attesting to the value of these teams. JCOA hosted one of the authors and provided access to its rich set of analyses and primary sources on Iraq in general and Task Force Freedom in particular.

[6] Bob Woodward, "Why Did the Violence Plummet? It Wasn't Just the Surge," *The Washington Post*, September 8, 2008.

[7] Joby Warrick and Robin Wright, "U.S. Teams Weaken Insurgency in Iraq," *The Washington Post*, September 6, 2008.

[8] Woodward, "Why Did the Violence Plummet?"

[9] *60 Minutes*, CBS News, September 7, 2008, available at <www.cbsnews.com/stories/2008/09/04/60minutes/main4415771_page3.shtml?tag=contentMain;contentBody>.

[10] In 2006, U.S. Pacific Command noted the revolutionary impact of interagency fusion cells. See Eric Hillard, "The Brain that Harnesses the Brawn of the War in Iraq," Pacific Air Forces Web site, December 7, 2006, available at <www.pacaf.af.mil/news/story.asp?id=123034479>. See also GEN Gary Luck, USA (Ret.), "Insights on Joint Operations: Art and Science," Joint Warfighting Center, U.S. Joint

Forces Command, September 2006, 33–34, and 2[d] edition (July 2008), 51.

[11] James Douglas Orton with Christopher J. Lamb, "Interagency National Security Teams: Can Social Science Contribute? *PRISM* 2, no. 2 (March 2011).

[12] For example, the Project on National Security Reform (PNSR) recommends placing a "hierarchy of decentralized teams" throughout the government to improve decisionmaking. *Forging a New Shield* (Arlington, VA: Center for the Study of the Presidency, 2008), 442–450. The Center for Strategic and International Studies "Beyond Goldwater-Nichols" report suggests using interagency teams to deal with complex contingencies. Clark Murdock et al., "Beyond Goldwater-Nichols: U.S. Government and Defense Reform for a New Strategic Era," Phase 2 Report (Washington, DC: Center for Strategic and International Studies, July 2005), 20–21.

[13] Although military researchers are well aware of the "fusion cell" experiences, the lessons learned have not been codified in doctrine, perhaps because the experience is so diverse and irregular. However, the U.S. Joint Forces Command, U.S. Special Operations Command, and U.S. Army have sponsored a handbook on interagency best practices: Lesa McComas, John Benson, Christopher Cook, Druso Daubon, and William McDaniel, "Interagency Teaming to Counter Irregular Threats," Johns Hopkins University Applied Physics Laboratory, Laurel, MD, Coordinating Draft, October 19, 2009.

[14] For example, the Civil Operations and Revolutionary Development Support (CORDS) program in Vietnam unified for the first time in 1967 the separate missions of the State Department, CIA, U.S. Agency for International Development, Department of Agriculture, and U.S. Information Service with the efforts of the Military Assistance Command, Vietnam. The CORDS program employed a wide range of assets against the enemy, shortened the decisionmaking cycle, improved unity of effort, and made it much easier to work with the Vietnamese government. Although CORDS proved to be extremely successful in combating the insurgency in Vietnam, its lessons were never institutionalized, and to this day the Provincial Reconstruction Teams in Afghanistan and Iraq suffer as a result. See *Forging a New Shield*, 559–560.

[15] James Jones, "The 21st Century Interagency Process," quoted in Laura Rozen, "New NSC Memo: Jones on the 21st Century Interagency Process," Foreign Policy Web site, April 6, 2009, available at <http://thecable.foreignpolicy.com/posts/2009/04/06/new_nsc_memo_jones_on_the_21st_century_interagency_process>.

[16] Christopher Lamb, "Three Pillars of Reform," in *Global Strategic Assessment 2009: America's Security Role in a Changing World*, ed. Hans Binnendijk and Patrick M. Cronin (Washington, DC: National Defense University Press, 2009).

[17] Robert M. Gates, remarks at The Nixon Center, February 24, 2010, available at <www.nixoncenter.org/index.cfm?action=showpage&page=2009-Robert-Gates-Transcript>.

[18] National Security Act of 1947, Title 1, Coordination for National Security, National Security Council, Section 101, available at <www.intelligence.gov/0-natsecact_1947.shtml#s101>.

[19] Ambassador Ryan Crocker, interview with JCOA staff and review of documents, December 8, 2009.

[20] See note 12.

[21] This section is based upon Orton.

[22] Martin Hoegl and Luigi Proserpio, "Team Member Proximity and Teamwork in Innovative

Projects," *Research Policy* 33, no. 8 (2004).

[23] Justin J.P. Jansen, Frans A.J. Van Den Bosch, and Henk W. Volberda, "Managing Potential and Realized Absorptive Capacity: How Do Organizational Antecedents Matter?" *Academy of Management Journal* 48, no. 6 (2005), 1001.

[24] Deborah G. Ancona and David F. Caldwell, "Demography and Design: Predictors of New Product Team Performance," in *Organization Science* 3, no. 3 (August 1992), 324.

[25] R.M.J. Wells, "The Product Innovation Process: Are Managing Information Flows and Cross-functional Collaboration Key?" *Academy of Management Perspectives* 22, no. 1 (February 2008), 59.

[26] *Forging a New Shield*, 444–449.

[27] Ibid., 443–444; Orton.

[28] *Forging a New Shield*, 443–444.

[29] U.S. Army Field Manual 3–05.102, *Army Special Operations Forces Intelligence* (Washington, DC: Headquarters Department of the Army, July 2001), available at <http://fas.org/irp/doddir/army/fm3-05-102.pdf?>.

[30] Interview with MAJ James "Pat" Work, Army Ranger commander and conventional force staff officer with experience in cross-functional teams and fusion cells in Afghanistan and Iraq, October 20, 2009. Depending on their career path, current status, and rank, U.S. Special Operations Command often prefers that SOF officers not be identified by name. Where possible and permitted by the interviewee and the Pentagon review process, we acknowledge the identity of those we interviewed. Otherwise, we simply describe their background.

[31] According to one source, there were "[A]bout 110 CIA officers and 316 Special Forces personnel, plus massive airpower." Bob Woodward, *Bush at War* (New York: Simon and Schuster, 2002), 314. See also Linda Robinson, *Masters of Chaos* (New York: PublicAffairs, 2004), 153–177.

[32] Peter Blaber, *The Men, the Mission, and Me: Lessons from a Former Delta Force Commander* (New York: Berkley Caliber, 2008), 230.

[33] Matthew F. Bogdanos, "Joint Interagency Cooperation: The First Step," *Joint Force Quarterly* 37 (2d Quarter, 2005), 11.

[34] Interview with LTG Jerry Boykin, former Commander of the John F. Kennedy Special Warfare Center and Deputy Undersecretary of Defense for Intelligence, October 21, 2009.

[35] Michael Smith, *Killer Elite* (New York: St. Martin's Press, 2007), 231.

[36] Bogdanos, 11.

[37] At about the same time, John Sylvester and David Petraeus, the commander and deputy for operations of Stabilization Forces in Bosnia, also created a joint interagency task force (JIATF) to track terrorist funding that drew together military and Embassy personnel as well as the Defense Intelligence Agency, National Security Agency, and international law enforcement, intelligence, and operational partners. Jeanne Hull, "'We're All Smarter than Any One of Us': The Role of Inter-Agency Intelligence Organizations in Combating Armed Groups," *Journal of International and Public Affairs* (2008), 37–38.

[38] Brian Montopoli, "Chart: Troop Levels in Afghanistan over the Years," CBS News Web site, available at <www.cbsnews.com/blogs/2009/12/01/politics/politicalhotsheet/entry5855314.shtml>.

[39] Interview with Lieutenant Colonel David Scott Doyle, Army Ranger with experience in cross-functional teams and fusion cells in Afghanistan and Iraq, October 19, 2009.

[40] Ibid.

[41] Ibid.

[42] Work interview.

[43] Doyle interview. Other disciplines, like information operations, also habitually segregated intelligence and operations to their disadvantage from the SOF perspective. Interview with SOF intelligence officer who also served on a JIATF, February 19, 2010.

[44] Mark Davis, "Operation *Anaconda*: Command and Confusion in Joint Warfare," master's thesis, School of Advanced Air and Space Studies, June 2004, 70, available at <www.insidedefense.com/secure/data_extra/pdf3/dplus2004_2754.pdf>.

[45] Richard Andres and Jeffrey Hukill, "*Anaconda*: A Flawed Joint Planning Process," *Joint Force Quarterly* 47 (Winter 2007), 137.

[46] Doyle interview.

[47] Interview with FBI Supervisory Special Agent with multiple deployments in support of Operation *Iraqi Freedom*, October 28, 2009. Military sources (such as LTC David Scott Doyle) agreed with this characterization.

[48] This trend persisted in Afghanistan until recently. See Christopher J. Lamb and Martin Cinnamond, *Unity of Effort: Key to Success in Afghanistan*, Strategic Forum 248 (Washington, DC: National Defense University Press, October 2009), available at <www.ndu.edu/inss/docUploaded/SF248_Lamb.pdf>.

[49] Interview with MAJ Richard Garey, Part II, Operational Leadership Experiences Project, Combat Studies Institute, Center for Army Lessons Learned, November 5, 2007. Cross-functional team (CFTs) also informally shared intelligence and lessons learned, and in some cases were formally linked together as well, a process facilitated by the fact that by 2004–2005 CFT leaders might be on their second or third deployment with a CFT. Interview with former task force member with CFT, Fusion Cell, and JIATF experience in Operations *Enduring Freedom* (OEF) and *Iraqi Freedom* (OIF), October 27, 2009.

[50] Doyle interview.

[51] Yee-Kuang Heng and Ken McDonagh, "The Other War on Terror Revealed: Global Governmentality and the Financial Action Task Force's Campaign against Terrorist Financing," *Review of International Studies* (2008), 554.

[52] Caleb Temple, Defense Intelligence Agency, testimony to the House Armed Services Subcommittee on Terrorism, Unconventional Threats, and Capabilities and House Financial Services Subcommittee on Oversight and Investigations, July 28, 2005.

[53] The Internal Revenue Service even assigned Criminal Investigation Agents to Iraq to help the effort. Testimony of Acting Assistant Secretary Daniel Glaser on Financing for the Iraqi Insurgency, July 28, 2005, available at <www.ustreas.gov/press/releases/js2658.htm>.

[54] Hull, 42.

[55] Interview with counterterrorism expert who served on three interagency task forces, April 6, 2010.

[56] Hull, 42.

[57] Interview with SOF Task Force intelligence officer who also served on a JIATF, February 19, 2010.

[58] Collocation with one such team made this easier. Interview with Tres Hurst, former Special

Forces officer with multiple deployments as an interagency team leader, November 13, 2009.

[59] Former task force member interview.

[60] Hurst interview.

[61] Doyle interview.

[62] Boykin interview.

[63] Former task force member interview.

[64] Interview with SOF flag officer, JCOA, February 23, 2009.

[65] Boykin interview.

[66] Interview with Senior Special Forces officer with service in Combined Joint Special Operations Task Force–Arabian Peninsula, March 16, 2010.

[67] Counterterrorism expert interview.

[68] SOF Task Force intelligence officer interview.

[69] Ibid.

[70] This point was made by several sources, including MAJ James Work, email to authors, April 12, 2010.

[71] Former task force member interview; Doyle interview.

[72] Former task force member interview.

[73] Sometimes the interagency teams were called "tailored task forces" by conventional forces.

[74] Commanded by David Petraeus, the 101st created an early successful JIATF in September 2003. Tasked with intelligence fusion, deconfliction, and coordinating coalition targeting, JIATF–Mosul was dominated by the 101st, which had the bulk of personnel and resources in the area. Between October 2003 and January 2004 when relieved by Task Force Olympia, JIATF–Mosul initiated "at least thirteen major joint operations." Hull, 40–41.

[75] Interview with Special Forces and Task Force Freedom operations officer, December 10, 2009.

[76] Daniel Gonzales et al., *Networked Forces in Stability Operations: 101st Airborne Division, 3/2 and 1/25 Stryker Brigades in Northern Iraq* (Santa Monica, CA: RAND, 2007), xxi–xxiii.

[77] "Mosul Stable, Stryker Battalion Rejoins Brigade," November 15, 2004, available at <www.strykernews.com/archives/2004/11/15/mosul_stable_stryker_battalion_rejoins_brigade.html>.

[78] Thanassis Cambanis, "U.S., Iraqi Troops Fight to Retake Control in Mosul," *Boston Globe*, November 17, 2004, available at <www.boston.com/news/world/articles/2004/11/17/us_iraqi_troops_fight_to_retake_control_in_mosul/>.

[79] Department of Defense, Special Defense Department Operational Update Briefing on Operations in Northwest Iraq, September 14, 2005, available at <www.defense.gov/transcripts/transcript.aspx?transcriptid=2109>.

[80] Robert Hulslander, "The Operations of Task Force Freedom in Mosul, Iraq: A Best Practice in Joint Operations," *JCOA Journal* 9, no. 3 (September 2007), 18–19.

[81] Interview with Special Forces and Task Force Freedom operations officer, December 10, 2009.

[82] Gonzales et al., 153.

[83] Special Forces and Task Force Freedom operations officer interview.

[84] See Robert Kaplan, "The Coming Normalcy?" *The Atlantic Monthly*, April 2006, available at

<www.theatlantic.com/doc/200604/coming-normalcy>.

[85] Gonzales et al., 70–71, 154.

[86] Special Forces and Task Force Freedom operations officer, email to authors, April 10, 2010.

[87] COL Robert Brown, video teleconference from Mosul to the 3/2 Stryker Brigade Combat Team Lessons Learned Conference, March 23, 2005.

[88] Division commanders had more intelligence, surveillance, and reconnaissance (ISR) and mobility assets, which were in short supply for conventional units (unlike the SOF Task Force). Also, conventional forces typically could only muster interagency representation at the division level. Interview with Army officer who served in the 10th Mountain Division in Afghanistan and was the operations officer for a Ranger CFT in Afghanistan and Iraq, October 26, 2009.

[89] Special Forces and Task Force Freedom operations officer interview.

[90] Gonzales et al., 113.

[91] JCOA, interview with Task Force Freedom G2, May 14, 2005, in "A Comprehensive Approach: Iraq Case Study," Powerpoint presentation, slide AN 3f.

[92] Hulslander, 19.

[93] Special Forces and Task Force Freedom operations officer interview.

[94] Ibid.

[95] ICITAP partners American law enforcement officials with host countries to professionalize local law enforcement institutions and build the rule of law. This emphasizes protecting human rights, fighting corruption, and eliminating transnational crime and terrorism. ICITAP partners with the Departments of State and Defense, U.S. Agency for International Development, and the Millennium Challenge Corporation. Special Forces and Task Force Freedom operations officer interview.

[96] Hurst interview.

[97] Special Forces and Task Force Freedom operations officer interview.

[98] MG Mike Flynn, quoted in Sean Naylor, "Afghanistan Insurgency Has Grown 10-fold," *Air Force Times*, November 3, 2009.

[99] JCOA, *The Comprehensive Approach: An Iraq Case Study*, 1.

[100] JCOA, "A Comprehensive Approach: Iraq Case Study," slide AN 2d.

[101] Lawrence Lewis, "High Value Individual Targeting and ISR in a Counterinsurgency: Operation *Iraqi Freedom*," JCOA, 2.

[102] Boykin interview.

[103] Doyle interview.

[104] George Packer, "The Lesson of Tal Afar," *The New Yorker*, April 20 2006, available at <www.newyorker.com/archive/2006/04/10/060410fa_fact2?currentPage=all>.

[105] Interview with BG H.R. McMaster, May 26, 2010.

[106] The 3d ACR also benefited from regimental commander COL H.R. McMaster's previous experience working in U.S. Central Command as the head of GEN John Abizaid's Commander's Advisory Group, a position that allowed him to meet with many unit commanders in Iraq between 2003 and 2004.

[107] See oral history interview with LTC Yingling for his explanation of the effects coordinator job: <http://cgsc.cdmhost.com/cdm4/item_viewer.php?CISOROOT=/p4013coll13&CISOPTR=273&REC=4>.

[108] McMaster interview.

[109] 3ᵈ Armored Cavalry Regimental History, available at <www.hood.army.mil/3d_acr/Unit%20 Lineage/Regimental%20History.aspx>.

[110] Former Special Forces officer and Task Force Freedom Operations Officer, email to authors, April 14, 2010.

[111] McMaster interview.

[112] Former Special Forces officer and Task Force Freedom Operations Officer, email to the authors, April 14, 2010.

[113] McMaster interview.

[114] Ricks, 60–61.

[115] McMaster interview.

[116] Ibid.

[117] Packer.

[118] Ricks, 59.

[119] Niel Smith and Sean MacFarland, "Anbar Awakens: The Tipping Point," *Military Review* (March–April 2008), 42.

[120] Interview with BG Sean MacFarland, March 9, 2010.

[121] Smith and MacFarland, 43.

[122] Interview with a flag officer who served as a field grade officer in Ramadi in 2006, March 9, 2010.

[123] MacFarland interview.

[124] Linda Robinson, *Tell Me How this Ends* (New York: PublicAffairs, 2008), 272.

[125] MacFarland interview.

[126] Ricks, 65.

[127] MacFarland interview.

[128] Smith and MacFarland, 50.

[129] MacFarland interview; Ricks, 69*ff*.

[130] Flag officer interview.

[131] MacFarland interview.

[132] Email from senior Special Forces officer, April 13, 2010.

[133] The phrase "networked-based targeting" is used in multiple sources, including "A Comprehensive Approach: Iraq Case Study."

[134] Ibid.

[135] Work, email.

[136] This point has been made with respect to Iraq and, more recently, Afghanistan. See, respectively: Richard H. Shultz, Jr., and Roy Godson, "Intelligence Dominance: A Better Way Forward in Iraq," *The Weekly Standard*, July 31, 2006, and MG Michael T. Flynn, Capt Matt Pottinger, and Paul D. Batchelor, "Fixing Intel: A Blueprint for Making Intelligence Relevant in Afghanistan," Center for a New American Security, January 2010, available at <www.cnas.org/files/documents/press/AfghanIntel_Flynn_Jan2010_code507_voices.pdf>.

[137] Michael Flynn, Rich Jergens, and Thomas Cantrell, "Employing ISR: SOF Best Practices,"

Joint Force Quarterly 50 (3ᵈ Quarter, 2008), 60.

[138] Ibid., 56.

[139] GEN Boykin made this point in our interview and elsewhere: 'We're trying to operationalize intelligence . . . to achieve the kind of synergy where our analysts are driving our collections. We caught Saddam Hussein because we had analysts putting a puzzle together where they were literally turning to operators across the room and saying, 'Here's what I need you to get.' The operator would then get the imagery or capture an individual and interrogate him and then feed that information directly back to the analysts, who would put that into the puzzle and say: 'OK, the next thing I need is the following.'" Smith, 261.

[140] Hillard.

[141] Sean Naylor, "SpecOps Unit Nearly Nabs Zarqawi," *Army Times*, April 26, 2006; Mark Bowden, "The Ploy: How the U.S. Military Cracked Al-Zarqawi's Inner Circle," *The Atlantic Monthly*, May 2007, 54; Michael Smith, Hala Jaber, and Sarah Baxter, "How Iraq's Ghost of Death Was Cornered," *The London Times*, June 11, 2006.

[142] Senior Special Forces officer interview.

[143] Robinson, *Tell Me How this Ends*, 164.

[144] GEN Raymond Odierno, in "A Comprehensive Approach: Iraq Case Study," slide 7d.

[145] Robinson, *Tell Me How this Ends*, 272.

[146] The Commander, U.S. Special Operations Command (USSOCOM), has testified to the efficacy of direct action missions providing a time and space for counterinsurgency operations to be successful. See ADM Eric T. Olson, Statement to the Senate Armed Services Committee regarding the Afghanistan-Pakistan Strategic Review, April 1, 2009.

[147] Based on discussions with JCOA staff and review of documents, December 8, 2009.

[148] Central Intelligence Agency Lessons Learned Program, "Operating an Interagency Task Force: The Experience of the CIA-led Foreign Fighter Task Force," 2008.

[149] JCOA, "A Comprehensive Approach: Iraq Case Study," slide AN 2c3.

[150] Orton.

[151] John Mathieu, M. Travis Maynard, Tammy Rapp, and Lucy Gilson, "Team Effectiveness 1997–2007: A Review of Recent Advancements and a Glimpse into the Future," *Journal of Management* 34, no. 3 (June 2008), 412–413.

[152] Susan E. Jackson, "Team Composition in Organizational Settings: Issues in Managing an Increasingly Diverse Work Force," in *Group Process and Productivity*, ed. Stephen Worchel, Wendy Wood, and Jeffrey Simpson (Newbury Park, CA: Sage Publications, 1992), 138–173.

[153] Jon Katzenbach and Douglas Smith, *The Wisdom of Teams: Creating the High Performance Organization* (Boston: Harvard Business School Press, 1993), 21.

[154] Ibid., 55.

[155] Ibid.

[156] Doyle interview.

[157] Former task force member interview; Hurst interview.

[158] U.S. Joint Forces Command, "Cross Functional Fusion Cells: Application of Tactical Fusion Cell Principles at Higher Echelons," Concept White Paper V 1.5 (January 8, 2008), 3.

[159] Hurst interview.

[160] One source with experience in multiple interagency groups over several decades believes interagency success is significantly higher in combat zones. Counterterrorism expert interview.

[161] Hull, 30–31.

[162] Doyle interview.

[163] Interview with Intelligence Community official, October 29, 2009. The Intelligence Community official noted that being in "injun" territory as opposed to the Green Zone also had a powerful and positive effect on collaboration.

[164] Senior Special Forces officer interview.

[165] Special Forces and Task Force Freedom operations officer interview.

[166] SOF Task Force intelligence officer interview.

[167] 10th Mountain Division officer interview.

[168] Counterterrorism expert interview.

[169] J.E. Mathieu, L.L. Gilson, and T.M. Ruddy, "Empowerment and Team Effectiveness: An Empirical Test of an Integrated Model," *Journal of Applied Psychology* 91 (2006), 97–108.

[170] Daniel R. Denison, Stuart L. Hart, and Joel A. Kahn, "From Chimneys to Cross-Functional Teams: Developing and Validating a Diagnostic Model," *Academy of Management Review* 39, no. 4 (1996), 1005–1023.

[171] Special Forces and Task Force Freedom operations officer interview.

[172] FBI Supervisory Special Agent interview; Boykin interview.

[173] SOF Task Force intelligence officer interview.

[174] Ibid.

[175] Christopher Fussell, Trevor Hough, and Matthew Pedersen, "What Makes Fusion Cells Effective," master's thesis, Naval Postgraduate School, December 2009.

[176] Interview with SOF flag officer, JCOA, January 14, 2009.

[177] Senior Special Forces officer interview.

[178] Glenn M. Parker, *Cross-Functional Teams: Working with Allies, Enemies, and Other Strangers* (San Francisco: Jossey-Bass, 2003), 271.

[179] Doyle interview.

[180] Former task force member interview.

[181] Special Forces and Task Force Freedom operations officer interview.

[182] 10th Mountain Division officer interview.

[183] Thomas Harris and John Sherblom, *Small Group and Team Communication* (Boston: Allyn and Bacon, 1999), 130.

[184] Geoffrey Bellman and Kathleen Ryan, *Extraordinary Teams: How Ordinary Teams Achieve Amazing Results* (New York: John Wiley and Sons, 2009), 18.

[185] Lewis, 13.

[186] Based on discussions with JCOA staff and review of documents.

[187] SOF flag officer interview.

[188] Interview with officer in charge of interagency coordination for USSOCOM and member of GEN Petraeus's staff in 2007–2008, October 26, 2009.

[189] Ambassador Crocker previously served in Afghanistan and Pakistan; GEN Petraeus served previously in Bosnia, and his first tour in Iraq, in Mosul, during and immediately following the invasion of Iraq had earned him high marks for his prescience in dealing with postconflict stabilization issues. Robinson, *Tell Me How this Ends*, 68*ff*.

[190] JCOA, *The Comprehensive Approach: An Iraq Case Study*, vol. 1, 6–7.

[191] Multinational Force–Iraq (MNF–I) Paper, "Counterinsurgency Guidance," September 16, 2007, in ibid., 18.

[192] Crocker interview and review of documents.

[193] JCOA interview with GEN David Petraeus, January 28, 2009, in "A Comprehensive Approach: Iraq Case Study," slide UE51.

[194] Jackson, 138–173.

[195] Former task force member interview.

[196] Senior Special Forces officer interview.

[197] J. Richard Hackman, "The Design of Work Teams," in *Handbook of Organizational Behavior*, ed. J.W. Lorsch (Englewood Cliffs, NJ: Prentice-Hall, 1987), 327.

[198] Jim Billington, "Three Essentials of an Effective Team," in *Teams that Click*, ed. Loren Gary et al. (Boston: Harvard Business School Publishing Corporation, 2004), 30–35.

[199] Robert D. Pritchard and Margaret D. Watson, "Understanding and Measuring Group Productivity," in *Group Process and Productivity*, 251–275.

[200] For example, 10th Mountain Division officer interview.

[201] Hurst interview.

[202] SOF flag officer interview.

[203] Hurst interview.

[204] Counterterrorism expert interview.

[205] Work interview.

[206] Hurst interview.

[207] Boykin interview.

[208] Counterterrorism expert interview.

[209] Special Forces and Task Force Freedom operations officer interview.

[210] James D. Thompson, *Organizations in Action* (New York: McGraw-Hill Book Company, 1967).

[211] Ibid., 62.

[212] Prescott C. Ensign, "Interdependence, Coordination, and Structure in Complex Organizations: Implications for Organization Design," *Mid-Atlantic Journal of Business*, March 1, 1998, available at <www.allbusiness.com/management/689725-1.html>.

[213] Work interview.

[214] Ian Brooks, *Organizational Behaviour: Individuals, Groups, and Organisation*, 3d ed. (Harrow: Pearson Education Limited, 2006), 99.

[215] JCOA interview with MNF–I CJ2, December 10, 2008.

[216] Interview with Intelligence Community official, October 29, 2009.

[217] Based on discussions with JCOA staff and review of documents.

[218] Former task force member interview.

[219] L. Argote, D. Gruenfeld, and C. Naquin, "Group Learning in Organizations," in *Groups at Work: Advances in Theory and Research*, ed. M.E. Turner (New York: Lawrence Erlbaum, 1999).

[220] William Metlay, Ira T. Kaplan, and Evelyn E. Rogers, "Self-Management in Context," in *Advances in Interdisciplinary Studies of Work Teams*, vol. 1, ed. Michael B. Beyerlein and Douglas A. Johnson (Greenwich, CT: JAI Press, 2001), 167–185.

[221] JCOA interview with former SOF Commander, February 23, 2009, in "A Comprehensive Approach: Iraq Case Study," slide UE6q.

[222] FBI Supervisory Special Agent interview.

[223] For example, at any given time, at least 10 percent of their hostage rescue personnel would be in Iraq.

[224] For example, 10th Mountain Division officer interview.

[225] The FBI personnel were also appreciated for their empowerment. They could make independent decisions and act more quickly than other personnel; even so, they were still limited in their freedom of action and were sometimes second-guessed by headquarters. Email from SOF Task Force intelligence officer, April 13, 2010.

[226] Hurst interview.

[227] Based on discussions with JCOA staff and review of documents, December 8, 2009.

[228] Counterterrorism expert interview.

[229] Ibid.; Hull.

[230] Special Forces and Task Force Freedom operations officer, email.

[231] Counterterrorism expert interview.

[232] 10th Mountain Division officer interview.

[233] Susan Albers Mohrman, Susan G. Cohen, and Allan M. Mohrman, *Designing Team Based Organizations: New Forms for Knowledge Work* (San Francisco: Jossey-Bass Publishers, 1995), 82–83; Parker, 136–137.

[234] Anne Marie Francesco and Barry Allen Gold, *International Organizational Behavior*, 2d ed. (Upper Saddle River, NJ: Pearson Education, 2005), 104.

[235] SOF flag officer interview.

[236] S.J. Zaccaro, A.L. Rittman, and M.A. Marks, "Team Leadership," *Leadership Quarterly* 12 (2001), 451–483.

[237] Reiner Huber et al., "Effects of Individual and Team Characteristics on the Performance of Small Networked Teams," *The International C2 Journal* 1, no. 1 (2007), 137–138.

[238] Hurst interview.

[239] Ricks, 72, 95.

[240] USSOCOM interagency coordination officer interview.

[241] JCOA, *The Comprehensive Approach: An Iraq Case Study*, 2.

[242] Unlike his predecessor, GEN Petraeus had the sense of perspective necessary for directing the high-value target teams. SOF Task Force intelligence officer interview.

[243] "SAS Kills Hundreds of Terrorists in 'Secret War' against al-Qaeda in Iraq," *London Telegraph*, August 30, 2008.

[244] Warrick and Wright.

[245] Ibid.

[246] Robinson, *Tell Me How this Ends*, 106.

[247] JCOA, *The Comprehensive Approach: An Iraq Case Study*, 5.

[248] Ibid., 9.

[249] Interview with MNF–I Deputy CJ5, October 30, 2008, in "A Comprehensive Approach: Iraq Case Study," slide AN1a3.

[250] For example, see Robinson, *Tell Me How this Ends*, 22.

[251] For example, Operation *Seventh Veil* was initiated by the 2d Brigade Combat Team in 2007 to investigate corrupt Iraqi soldiers and civil servants in northwest Baghdad. By properly investigating criminal allegations, the 2d BCT increased Iraqi government accountability and gained valuable intelligence on illegal militias and weapons trafficking as well as other criminal activities by Iraqi officials. "Operation Seventh Veil: Malign Officials and the Rule of Law," Best Practices in Counterinsurgency Case Study #1, Institute for the Study of War, April 1, 2010.

[252] Senior Special Forces officer interview.

[253] Gonzales et al., xxxi.

[254] *The Comprehensive Approach: An Iraq Case Study*, 9.

[255] Ibid.

[256] Work, email.

[257] Department of Defense, "Measuring Stability and Security in Iraq: Report to Congress," September 2008.

[258] Hurst interview.

[259] Former task force member interview.

[260] Ibid.; interview with Intelligence Community official, October 29, 2009.

[261] Hurst interview.

[262] For example, memoranda of understanding have been created to clarify the purpose of SOF liaisons around Washington. Discussions with Pentagon authorities responsible for oversight of special operations, May 3, 2010.

[263] Hurst interview.

[264] Barry Harris, "Stabilizing Iraq Provides Intelligence Lessons for Afghanistan," *The Cutting Edge*, June 15, 2009, available at <www.thecuttingedgenews.com/index.php?article=11396&pageid=20&pagename=Security>.

[265] MG Michael Flynn notes, "Virtually the only customers for the Fusion Centers' enemy-centric analyses are special operations forces focused on kill-and-capture missions." Flynn, Pottinger, and Batchelor, 22.

[266] Paul Lushenko, "Partnership 'Till It Hurts': The Use of Fusion Cells to Establish Unity of Effort Between SOF (Yin) and Conventional Forces (Yang)," *Small Wars Journal* (May 2010).

[267] Senior intelligence officer responsible for Iraq, 2008; JCOA meeting notes, author visit, December 8–9, 2010.

[268] Woodward, "Why Did the Violence Plummet?"

[269] RADM Edward Winters, head of Naval Special Warfare Command, recently acknowledged

the importance of "cross functional or multidiscipline intelligence teams," noting, "The comprehensive assimilation of intelligence disciplines into a single targeting element and its complete integration under tactical assault forces create[s] a powerful synergy unachievable through traditional stovepiped intelligence silos." Edward Winters, "Adapting Across the Spectrum of Conflict," *Joint Force Quarterly* 56 (1st Quarter, 2010), 78. See also Fussell, Hough, and Pedersen, and an unpublished paper by Mark Schafer and Christopher Fussell, "The Role of [SOF] in Counterinsurgency," Naval Postgraduate School. Both Schafer and Fussell are U.S. Navy SEAL officers with multiple OEF and OIF deployments. They explain why SOF activities must be fastidiously integrated with broader counterinsurgency efforts, and how "only effective coordination can ensure that counter-network operations are properly focused on the goal of providing space in which larger forces can execute the highly complex mission of counterinsurgency.

[270] Former task force member interview; SOF Task Force intelligence officer interview.

[271] See Sharon Weinberger, "What Is Woodward's 'Secret Weapon' in Iraq?" *Wired* Web site, September 9, 2008, available at <www.wired.com/dangerroom/2008/09/whats-the-milit/>.

[272] Work interview.

[273] Senior Special Forces officer interview.

About the Authors

Dr. Christopher J. Lamb is a Distinguished Research Fellow in the Center for Strategic Research, Institute for National Strategic Studies (INSS), at the National Defense University. He conducts research on national security strategy, policy, and organizational reform, and on defense strategy, requirements, plans, and programs. In 2008, Dr. Lamb was assigned to lead the Project for National Security Reform study of the national security system, which led to the 2008 report, *Forging a New Shield*. Prior to joining INSS in 2004, Dr. Lamb served as the Deputy Assistant Secretary of Defense for Resources and Plans where he had oversight of war plans, requirements, acquisition, and resource allocation matters for the Under Secretary of Defense (Policy). Previously, he served as Deputy Director for Military Development on the State Department's Interagency Task Force for Military Stabilization in the Balkans; Director of Policy Planning in the Office of the Assistant Secretary of Defense for Special Operations and Low-Intensity Conflict; and from 1985 to 1992 as a Foreign Service Officer in Haiti and Ivory Coast. Dr. Lamb is the author of numerous publications, including *United States Special Operations Forces*, coauthored with Dr. David Tucker, Naval Postgraduate School.

Mr. Evan Munsing is a Subject Matter Expert in the Center for Strategic Research, Institute for National Strategic Studies, at the National Defense University. Mr. Munsing is a graduate of Bard College at Simon's Rock and the London School of Economics and Political Science. He worked at the Center for Strategic Research from 2009 to 2010, where he conducted research on national security organizational performance. He is currently attending Marine Corps Officer Candidate School.